GANGSTER QUEEN BONNIE PARKER

AND OTHER MURDEROUS WOMEN OF MISSOURI

LARRY WOOD

Published by The History Press
An imprint of Arcadia Publishing
Charleston, SC
www.historypress.com

Front cover: Bonnie Parker, in one of many photos developed from film left behind in a Joplin apartment. *Public domain.*
Back cover, top to bottom: Prosecutor Roy McGee confronts Louise Myers with the bottle of poison she used to kill her husband. *Author's collection*; Lulu Prince Kennedy in her cell after her arrest. *From the Kansas City Times*; Ada Lee Biggs takes the stand to testify in her own defense. *Author's collection.*

First published 2026

Manufactured in the United States

ISBN 9781467170925

Library of Congress Control Number applied for

CONTENTS

PREFACE

Throughout history, most notorious murders have been committed by men. Men, by nature, tend to be more aggressive than women. Not only do men kill more often than women, but also the two sexes tend to kill for different reasons or under different circumstances.

When men kill, greed is often the motive. They often kill strangers. They often kill in public places and often while intoxicated or under the influence of drugs. Men sometimes kill just for the thrill of it.

On the other hand, when women kill, the act is more often in response to being abused or wronged by a partner. Women who kill are more likely to do so in private, intimate situations, and their victim is usually someone they know. And when they do kill for reasons other than personal grievance, passion, or self-defense, their participation is often as an accessory at the behest of a lover and not as the primary perpetrator.

Women serial killers or women who kill out of pure malevolence are rare. I can think of only a handful of such women in Missouri history, and I have written about a few of them. One who comes to mind is Bertha Gifford, whom I wrote about in *Wicked Women of Missouri* (The History Press, 2016). A Catawissa farmwife, Bertha was convicted of poisoning three children in the early 1900s, charged with homicide in two other cases, and suspected in as many as seventeen deaths in total.

But as I say, she was an exception to the rule. Most of the women whose stories are chronicled in this book killed in intimate situations, either in response to a perceived threat or wrong or else out of passion. Many of their stories caused a buzz and made headlines at the time the crimes were committed, but the sensation has since faded into the shadows of history. That many of these stories have not remained in the public consciousness, however, makes them no less fascinating. Often, I find the lesser-known cases to be at least as interesting as the well-known ones.

One of the few stories in this book that does not fit the mold of a woman killing in an intimate situation is that of Bonnie Parker. It also happens to be one of the few stories in the book that is still in the public consciousness, and because of the romantic legend that surrounds her and Clyde Barrow, it likely will remain there for the foreseeable future. Even Bonnie's story, though, does not contradict my general observations about why women kill. It's not known for sure that Bonnie ever killed a single person with her own hand, and although she may have enjoyed the thrill of the gangster life, she no doubt went along as an accomplice to Clyde's many murders more out of love for him and a desire to please him than for any other reason.

ACKNOWLEDGEMENTS

Gone are the days when a researcher had to drive hundreds of miles to access newspaper collections, census records, or other historical documents. Many such documents are now online, and more continue to be digitized and made available on the internet almost every week, it seems.

So, most of my research for this book was done at home sitting in front of a computer screen. I, therefore, came into direct contact with fewer people than I would have in the old days and have fewer people to thank. Most of my visits to libraries, archives, or museums were done virtually, and even when I placed a specific research request, many of those requests were fulfilled anonymously by someone identified only as "staff."

However, I do want to thank those staff members, and I do also have a couple of individuals I want to recognize by name. I particularly want to mention the reference department of the Missouri State Archives. The archives reference employees fulfilled numerous requests for state penitentiary records and mug shots. I also want to thank the reference section of the Joplin Public Library, which fulfilled several interlibrary loan requests for me.

I appreciate the support and encouragement I received from Joe Gartrell, acquisitions editor at The History Press, as I was researching and writing this book, and copy editor Abigail Fleming did an outstanding job of editing the manuscript.

1
YOU POKE ME AND I'LL POKE YOU
THE STORY OF MARY BALL

Shortly after midnight on December 12, 1867, a man, accompanied by another man, came into Leitch's Drugstore at the corner of Fourth and Olive Streets in downtown St. Louis "in a very battered condition." Bleeding from an ugly wound on the right side of his head, the injured man said he'd just come from a house on Seventh Street between Green and Washington Avenues where a woman had hit him in the head with a poker. He identified himself as Charles Rannells, a steamboat engineer on the Mississippi River, but he did not know the woman's name and did not want her arrested. A clerk in the drugstore summoned a doctor, who dressed the man's wound and pronounced it not dangerous.[1]

That's all that was reported at the time, but as it turned out, there was a lot more to the story.

After getting his wound dressed, the man calling himself Rannells and his partner went back to the "house" on Seventh Street and asked the madam if they could spend the night, as they could not get into the boardinghouse where they'd been staying. She told them they could, but the young woman who'd struck Rannells with the poker stayed in a different room and did not talk to them. The next morning, Rannells was feeling bad, and he was taken to the City Hospital, where, after a few days, his case was pronounced hopeless. Throughout his stay in the hospital, Rannells steadfastly refused to provide additional information about his assailant beyond what he'd already said.

Near the same time that doctors deemed Rannells beyond help, a young woman who was jailed at the city calaboose gave information that Lou Moulton was the woman who had struck the gravely wounded man, and Moulton was arrested. The informant said an old feud existed between Moulton and the injured man and that Moulton had struck him when he came to her place and began abusing her.[2]

Rannells died on December 21, yet later that same day, a man appeared at the police station and said he was the person Moulton had struck. Police did not lend credence to his story, and Moulton remained in jail awaiting further developments. A St. Louis newspaper told its readers, "The matter is still surrounded with some mystery."[3]

An investigation revealed that the man who claimed to be the victim whom Moulton had struck in the head with a poker on the night in question was telling the truth. However, he was not the man the girl at the house on Seventh Street between Green and Washington had struck. In an odd coincidence, two different men had been struck by pokers by two different women in downtown St. Louis on the same night. The assault committed by Lou Moulton had resulted only in superficial wounds, and she was released.[4]

Further investigation revealed that the fatal assault had been committed by "a colored prostitute" named Mary Ball in a house of ill repute at 611 Seventh Street that was run by Carrie Martin, another Black woman. It was also learned that the real name of the man Mary had attacked was Charles Ross, not Charles Rannells, and his companion was the riverboat man, while Ross was actually a railroad brakeman. No doubt Ross had been reluctant to reveal his true identity or that of his assailant, at least partly because he did not want it publicly known that he'd frequented a house of ill repute, particularly one occupied by Black women.[5]

Mary Ball was arrested on January 1, 1868, and a coroner's inquest into the circumstances of Ross's death was conducted on January 3. Testifying before the coroner's jury, Mary admitted that she had struck Ross, but she felt justified in doing so because he had been beating and choking her. Mary said she was in the back room of the house on Seventh Street on the night in question when Mary Wilson, another occupant of the house, brought in two men. One of them came into the back room where Mary Ball was, while the other stayed in the front room with the Wilson woman.[6]

After a while, Ross told Mary Ball to knock on the door to the other room and find out how much longer his partner was going to be. When Mary told Ross it was not her "business to knock at other people's doors,"

An Engineer Assaulted by a Woman.—Mr. Charles Rannells, a steamboat engineer, was taken into Leitch's drug store on Fourth street, yesterday morning, in a very battered condition. An ugly wound was bleeding on the side of his head. He stated that he went into a house on Seventh street, between Green and Washington avenue, early this morning, when a woman therein, without ceremony, struck him on the head with a poker. He doesn't know who she is, but he strongly protested against her arrest.' He was taken to the Williams House, and Dr. McDowell dressed his wound.

Mary Ball's killing of one of her "patrons" barely made the news in St. Louis newspapers. *From the St. Louis Daily Missouri Democrat.*

he grew angry and called her names. He started choking her and upset the chair she was sitting in. He then started beating her while she was on the floor. Ross's partner appeared at the door, and when Ross got up and started walking away, Mary picked up a nearby poker and hurled it at him. Just as he reached the door to the other room, the poker hit him in the head with enough force that the pointed end stuck in the side of his head. Ross pulled the poker out of his head himself, and Mary Wilson held a towel to his head to stop the bleeding. Ross and his partner then went away, laughing about the matter. Mary Ball said she threw the poker as an angry reaction but did not mean to hurt the man.[7]

The testimony of Carrie Martin, who was in the back room with Mary Ball and Charles Ross at the time of the incident, generally confirmed what Mary had said, except that Carrie portrayed Mary as more nonchalant about the whole affair than Mary had let on to the jury. She said that when Mary Wilson told Mary Ball that she should be ashamed of herself for what she did, Mary Ball did not appear sorry for what had happened and said that she would do the same thing to anybody else who mistreated her. When a doctor who examined Ross on the morning after the incident said that Mary must have been trying to kill the man, she said she didn't care whether she killed him or not.[8]

Mary Wilson also took the stand and basically corroborated what Carrie Martin had said. The jury returned a verdict that Ross had come to his death "by a wound in the head inflicted by an iron poker thrown by Mary Ball," and Mary was committed for trial.[9]

Mary's preliminary examination began on January 20. Testimony was essentially the same as that given at the coroner's inquest. According to one report, Mary appeared indifferent to the outcome of the hearing and seemed "more anxious to display her red Morocco gaiters than listen to the proceedings." During the examination, the defense tried to make hay out of the fact that two different men had been struck with pokers by two different women on the same night. Not only was the identity of the body at the coroner's inquest in doubt, but also no solid proof existed that the subject of the inquest was killed by Mary Ball. Therefore, she should not be charged with the murder of Charles Ross. When the examination concluded on January 25, however, Mary was bound over to await the action of a grand jury, and she was remanded to jail in lieu of a $2,000 bond.[10]

Mary was charged with first-degree manslaughter in early April, but her case was continued until late September. On October 1, she was convicted of manslaughter in the fourth degree and sentenced to two years in the penitentiary. In April 1870, based partly on her good conduct while imprisoned, she was released and granted a full pardon after serving three-fourths of her sentence.[11]

2

UNLAWFULLY INTIMATE

THE STORY OF MARTHA TAYLOR

On Sunday morning, July 22, 1876, Sam Smith, standing on the north bank of the Missouri River in southern Warren County, Missouri, spotted a man's body floating slowly down the river in the shallow waters near the bank. Smith summoned help, and the body was brought to shore, where Justice of the Peace F.W. Schneider, aided by a local doctor, conducted a postmortem examination.[12]

The body was identified as that of Samuel Taylor, a thirty-eight-year-old man who lived nearby in a shanty on the banks of the river with his twenty-eight-year-old wife, Martha, and one child. Taylor was described as a man of "rather loose habits and of very weak mind." Although he was white, he was known to associate mainly with his Black neighbors. The initial examination revealed two wounds to Taylor's body, one on his left temple and one on the left side of his neck, but a definite cause of death could not be ascertained.[13]

Further inspection revealed a third wound below the left eye, and all three wounds appeared to have been made by an instrument that was sharp on one edge and blunt on the other, such as the blade of a large pocketknife. Although the initial examination had been inconclusive, authorities now felt that Taylor was killed by some unknown party.[14]

Suspicion soon settled on Dan Price, a thirty-three-old Black man who was a close associate of Taylor. He and Taylor ran a trotline in partnership, and they often fished and hunted together. Since the death of Price's wife in mid-1875, he had frequently visited the Taylor home.[15]

Rumors that circulated in the late spring and early summer of 1876, however, had put a strain on the friendship between the two men. It was whispered around the neighborhood that Price was "unlawfully intimate" with Taylor's wife. Price denied the rumors, but Taylor was still disturbed by them. Despite the strain on their relationship, the two men remained associates.[16]

However, the questionable relationship between Price and Martha Taylor, as reported by their neighbors, was enough to cast suspicion on them after Taylor's death, and the fact that Price was found staying at Mrs. Taylor's home when law officers went looking for them did little to allay such suspicion. Price and his paramour were both arrested on August 4 and taken before Justice Schneider for examination. This was the same man who had conducted the postmortem on Taylor's body.[17]

Several Black men testified at the hearing. Jack Ousley said he'd had a conversation with Price in the small community of Holstein a few days after Taylor's body was taken from the river and that Price told him Mrs. Taylor was "going on" about her husband's death and he didn't know what to do about it. Ousley said he told Price that if he didn't have anything to do with the death, he needn't worry about it, but Price didn't seem pacified by this reassurance. Richard "Uncle Dick" Hurt, who stayed at the Price home on the night Taylor disappeared, testified that Price left that evening with the stated intention of going squirrel hunting; uncharacteristically, he stayed out all night and did not have any squirrels when he returned the next morning. Sam Smith, the man who found Taylor's body, testified that he'd heard Price say that Taylor was jealous because he thought Price and Martha were too intimate. Major Edwards testified that, in conversation with Price about a week before Taylor was killed, Price told him that Taylor had been talking about the alleged intimacy between his wife and Price and that the talk had to stop. Edwards told Price that Sam Taylor had a big mouth but that he wouldn't hurt anybody. Price insisted that Edwards didn't know what "a damn rascal" Taylor was, that he meant to make the man stop talking, and that Edwards shouldn't be surprised to hear of Taylor's death."[18]

Next to testify was Martha Taylor. She and her husband were known to engage in frequent arguments and occasionally in "rough and tumble brawls," and she admitted that they had argued in the late afternoon of July 20, because she'd gone shopping and forgotten to purchase coal oil, which he'd told her to get. After the argument, Taylor left, saying he was going down to the river to go fishing and that he might not be back until the next day. The next time she saw him was when he was being taken out of the river

THE TAYLOR MURDER IN WARREN COUNTY.

Damaging Evidence Against the Wife of the Murdered Man.

A White Woman and a Negro Paramour

As this headline suggests, Martha Taylor's involvement with a "Negro paramour" was considered almost as scandalous as her conspiracy to kill her husband. *From the St. Louis Republican.*

on the morning of the July 22. Martha said her husband and Dan Price had quarreled several times in the past but that they'd not had any difficulties lately and, in fact, had been good friends.[19]

Testifying in his own defense, Price explained why he'd stayed out all night and come home without any squirrels. He said he didn't find any squirrels, so he decided to go fishing. He caught a few small fish but threw them back. After baiting his trotline, he built a fire, lay down, and fell asleep. Price admitted having the conversation with Major Edwards about Taylor's "going on" concerning the rumors of his wife's infidelity. However, Price said he did not threaten to kill Taylor as Edwards implied. Instead, Price said he told Edwards that Taylor had threatened to kill some of the gossipers and Price had merely added that Taylor might be the one who got killed if he didn't quit talking so much.[20]

At the end of the examination, Schneider dismissed the case against Mrs. Taylor for lack of evidence, and she was released. Price, on the other hand, was bound over on a charge of first-degree murder, taken to Warrenton that very day, and lodged in the Warren County Jail to await the action of a grand jury.[21]

After her discharge, Martha Taylor stayed close to home for the first week or so and then boarded a steamboat headed up the Missouri River.

After she'd left the area, additional evidence against her in the death of her husband came to light, and a deputy sheriff and another man went out in search of her. She was located in the Little Bear Creek Hills in the extreme southwestern part of Warren County, brought back to Warrenton, and lodged in jail there on August 17.[22]

When Mrs. Taylor was brought into court for her preliminary examination on August 23, she was described as "tall and slender" with "dark hair and eyes, low forehead," and wearing a black calico dress. At first, she was quiet and had little to say, but when the testimony of the witnesses began to incriminate her in her husband's death, she "became restless, would denounce some of the statements as 'lies,' and immediately after commence humming some religious tune and walk to and fro in the court-room."[23]

The primary additional evidence against Mrs. Taylor proved to be the testimony of Price's sixteen-year-old daughter, Maggie. Miss Price said she'd once overheard Martha and her father talking about "putting Taylor out of the way." On another occasion, Martha had told her that her father was going to "put Sam out of the way" and that Martha was "glad of it." Even more incriminating was Maggie's statement that her father and Taylor had left together on the evening of July 20 and that, when her father returned the next morning, he spoke to Mrs. Taylor, who later told Maggie that her father had gotten rid of Sam. Specifically, Martha said Price had hit Taylor on the side of the head with a gun while he was standing on the bank of the Missouri River, threw him in the river, and watched him sink. Maggie added further that Martha had told her she and her father were planning to get married once they were clear of Sam Taylor. Maggie said she'd stayed with the Taylors throughout the summer and that her father came back to Martha's house after the killing, stayed there that night, and continued to stay there until he was arrested. Maggie said Martha Taylor had threatened to kill her if she told what she knew.[24]

Another new witness was Parks Gardener, a young Black man who gave testimony of "criminal intimacy" between Price and Mrs. Taylor, but the *Warrenton Banner* felt that the details were too salacious to "give publicity to in this paper." A later report suggested that Gardener, while on his way to the river, had seen the couple "lying behind the hen house in amorous relations."[25]

Most of the rest of the testimony at Martha's preliminary hearing was a repetition of or an expansion on what had been presented at Price's prelim. "Uncle Dick" Hurt, however, related a substantially different version of what he'd said earlier. Instead of Price coming back to his own place on the morning after Taylor's disappearance, as Hurt had said the first time, he now testified that he thought Price had gone back to the Taylor residence late the previous evening and had spent the night there. Hurt said that when he went over to the Taylor residence early on the morning of July 21 and knocked on the door, Price was not there, but Hurt said he saw Price coming up the road soon afterward and he was pretty sure that, when he'd knocked on the door, Price had jumped out the window and was trying to fool him into thinking he'd been out all night. When Price left to get some chickens, Mrs. Taylor had confirmed that Price had spent the night with her.[26]

What action was taken at the conclusion of Martha's preliminary hearing is unclear from available sources, but the evidence suggests she was charged as an accessory to murder and let out on bond to await trial.

On the night of October 14, Dan Price escaped from the Warren County Jail along with two white men charged with burglary. Price was described as "a large man, very black, six feet high, and had on a cheap calico shirt torn up the back." The sheriff offered a reward of $150 for Price's recapture. A few days later, Missouri Governor Charles H. Hardin issued a proclamation adding $300 to the reward.[27]

For about a week after his escape, Price remained in his home territory, where Martha Taylor helped harbor and conceal him. Around October 20, he fled the vicinity when his pursuers began to close in on him. He was located and arrested in Alton, Illinois, on October 29 and brought back to Warren County, where a joint indictment was issued against him and Martha Taylor. As principal in the crime, Price was charged with first-degree murder, and Martha, as an accessory before the fact, was charged with second-degree murder.[28]

Price was then taken to neighboring St. Charles County and lodged in jail there for safekeeping. Price's case was severed from Mrs. Taylor's, and his case came up first. He was brought back to Warrenton for trial beginning on November 20. The prosecution presented evidence similar to what had been produced at the coroner's jury and the preliminary examination. The most significant difference was that the state now maintained that Price had killed Taylor in the Taylor home and dragged his body to the river instead of killing him on the bank of the river as testimony during the prior proceedings had suggested. On November 22, the jury found the defendant guilty of first-degree murder after only ten minutes of deliberation. Sentenced to hang in January 1877, Price was returned to the St. Charles County Jail to await the execution.[29]

Martha Taylor's trial began almost immediately after Price's ended. She was found guilty of murder in the second degree and sentenced to twenty-five years in the state penitentiary. Before being conveyed to the state prison on November 27, she was interviewed by a reporter from the local *Warrenton Banner*.[30]

Martha said she was born in neighboring Montgomery County and had lived in the area her whole life. She'd married Taylor about nine years ago and had lived with him ever since except for one time about three years earlier when Taylor had been accused of horse thievery by some of his neighbors and threatened with violence if he didn't leave the territory. Taylor had stayed gone about a year, and when he came back, he and Martha moved to the Pinckney/Holstein area.[31]

Martha said Taylor treated her kindly at times but could be "very rough" at other times. She complained that they had very little to live on and that she earned most of the money they did have by taking in sewing. "My husband is to blame a great deal for my degradation," she said. "He brought me down into that neighborhood, and we had only negroes for our associates."[32]

Martha found little fault with most of the testimony given at the legal proceedings against her and Price. She made it clear, however, that she was not present when her husband was killed. He left on Thursday evening, just as the initial testimony indicated, and she did not see him again until he was dragged out of the river on Saturday morning. She admitted that Price did come back to her house early Friday morning and stayed with her each night after that until he was arrested.[33]

She claimed she never told Maggie, Price's daughter, or anyone else that she planned to marry Price, and she also denied telling Maggie that she would kill her if she ever told what she knew. Instead, Martha had told Maggie that her father had threatened to kill her if she talked. Martha also took issue with the testimony of Parks Gardener, the young man who'd testified that he'd seen Martha and Price in an act of sexual intimacy behind the henhouse. Gardener, Martha said, was the only witness who'd flat-out lied in his testimony against her.[34]

When Martha was processed in at the state penitentiary later in the day on November 27, she was described as standing five feet, five inches tall, with auburn hair, hazel eyes, and fair complexion.[35]

Dan Price was brought back to Warrenton from St. Charles and executed on schedule on January 18, 1877. Maintaining his innocence until the very end, Price mounted the steps to the scaffold "with but little show of nervousness" and danced in the air shortly after 9:00 a.m.[36]

In mid-April 1882, Martha Taylor received a full pardon from acting governor Alexander Campbell and was released on the seventeenth after serving less than five and a half years of her twenty-five-year term. A report at the time said Martha had been confined in the prison hospital with rheumatism for the previous four years and that her conduct had been exemplary. The pardon had been recommended by the prison matron and other officials, including the chaplain. Martha had living parents who had expressed a willingness to take care of her; presumably, she went to stay with them on her release.[37]

3

ALICE DYKE

COLD-BLOODED MURDERER OR SELF-DEFENDER?

Who are you going to believe? Inhabitants of "a resort for the lowest kind of harlots" or the companions of a young real estate agent from a "highly respected" family who was killed at the ill-famed resort? That was the question that faced residents of Kansas City when they awoke on July 31, 1887, and began to peruse the Sunday morning newspaper.[38]

Earlier that morning, shortly after midnight, a shot had rung out in the vicinity of Fifth and Penn Streets in downtown Kansas City, disturbing "the stillness of the midnight hour." Startled by the sound, neighbors and a few "stragglers who were homeward bound" rushed to the scene to learn the cause of the commotion. A young man, soon identified as twenty-six-year-old John Hamilton, lay dying in the doorway of a brothel or "saloon" at 449 West Fifth Street.[39]

His companions, W.W. Fristoe and John Wright, told similar stories. The three men had been passing along the street when they saw a white woman, later identified as twenty-seven-year-old Alice Dyke, standing in the front doorway of the house. Hamilton called to the woman, "Hello! Howdy do this evening?"

"You'd better go on, you God damned son of a bitch," the woman snapped.

"Don't get cranky," Hamilton said.

Without another word, Dyke rushed up to the man, pointed a .32-caliber pistol within inches of his face, and pulled the trigger. The bullet struck him in the corner of the right eye, and he collapsed to the sidewalk mortally wounded. The woman screamed, "Oh, my God, he's shot!" She told his companions to hold his head until she got some water, and then she raced back into the house. Two other young women who lived in the house dashed outside, screaming in panic, as Alice returned with a pitcher of water.

Both of Hamilton's companions claimed that they didn't know the woman and that the shooting was entirely unprovoked.[40]

Shortly after the shooting, a patrol wagon arrived and transported Hamilton to the central police station, where an examination revealed that the bullet had entered between the right eye and the bridge of the nose and ranged downward. The forehead and right cheek were powder burned, showing the shot had been fired at close range. "All attempts to stop the flow of the crimson fluid were futile," and Hamilton died at 12:44 a.m., "the victim of a lewd woman's furious passion."[41]

After delivering Hamilton to the police station, the patrol wagon returned to the scene of the crime, and officers arrested Alice Dyke and the other two occupants of her house. They were conveyed to the police station, where reporters from Kansas City newspapers interviewed them.[42]

One of Dyke's boarders was a white girl, about eighteen years of age, named Minnie Hall. The other was a Black girl, about the same age, who said she was generally known as Mattie McKinney but that her proper name was Mattie Johnson. Mattie wanted it known that she was employed as a chambermaid in Alice's house and "worked honestly for her money."[43]

Although both girls were in the house and heard the fatal shot fired, neither one of them directly witnessed the incident. They agreed, however, that they had heard a commotion at the front door, as if someone was trying to break in, prior to the sound of the gunfire and that a man who looked like the deceased had visited their house a few hours before the shooting. The visitor ordered a bottle of soda and gave Minnie Hall a quarter for it, and he became upset when she returned only fifteen cents, claiming he was being overcharged. Threatening to "have the house pulled and to do up Minnie" before the night was over, he stormed out.[44]

Minnie admitted that she had given Alice the weapon with which she shot Hamilton. She said Alice had wanted it for protection because she had about $450 in the house and thought someone might try to steal the money. Minnie had borrowed the gun from a male friend of hers, and she was concerned that she or her friend might be blamed for the shooting.[45]

Although Alice Dyke was the suspect's real name, she was known by numerous aliases, including Alice Drake, Alice White, Alice Hopkins, and Alice Chapman. A plump blond woman, she had lived in Kansas City much of her life but had only recently returned to the city after a brief residence in Leavenworth, Kansas. The *Kansas City Times* said she was "anything but a beauty," and the *Kansas City Journal* agreed that she was "by no means good looking." The *Times* claimed she had a "hardened expression which pervades every feature of her countenance" and "betokens a long acquaintanceship with vice." Her vicious appearance was "not softened by a pair of steel gray eyes through which she glared out of the prison cell like an imprisoned tigress." When asked to tell her side of the story, Alice "shut her lips down in a determined manner" and refused even to admit that she had shot Hamilton. She said she had nothing to say until she saw a lawyer.[46]

Although Alice refused to make a statement for publication, she did end up talking to the police chief. Echoing what Minnie and Mattie had told reporters, Alice said the man she shot had been to her house two or three times on Saturday evening. On his last visit, he had gone away angry and uttering threats over a dispute about the cost of a bottle of pop. Shortly after midnight, he returned, kicked at her door, and was using "insulting and profane language." Feeling threatened, she shot him in what she thought was self-defense.[47]

In reporting Alice's statement to the police chief, the *Kansas City Journal* observed that she was "well known to the police." At one time, she "lived with a negro to whom she claimed to be married." Alice had "been arrested frequently for disturbing the peace, being an inmate of disreputable houses, and on other charges."[48]

Both Minnie Hall and Mattie Johnson were released on Sunday morning after questioning, as were Hamilton's companions, Wright and Fristoe.[49]

A coroner's inquest was held over Hamilton's body on Monday, August 1. Fristoe admitted that he, Hamilton, and Wright had visited a saloon in the vicinity of Alice Dyke's place early Saturday night, where they had purchased and drunk some soda pop, but he suggested that it was not the same house where the shooting took place. Minnie Hall reaffirmed her testimony that she heard kicking at the door of Alice's house prior to the shooting, but she couldn't be certain that the man Alice shot was the same man who had caused a disturbance earlier in the evening over the cost of the pop. At the conclusion of the inquest, the jury returned a verdict charging Alice Dyke with felonious assault resulting in death and recommended that she be held for further examination.[50]

On September 15, a grand jury indicted Alice for murder in the first degree. She pleaded not guilty at her arraignment a few days later, and her trial date was set for October 17.[51]

Alice Dyke, sketched at the time of her arrest (*left*) and at the time of her trial (*right*). *From the Kansas City Journal.*

At the start of her trial a month later, the defense asked for a continuance based on the fact that a potential witness was missing, but the request was denied. When Alice was brought into the courtroom on October 20 for the first day of testimony, she appeared, according to the *Kansas City Journal*, "utterly oblivious of the fact that she was to be tried for one of the seemingly least provoked and most inexcusable murders known in the annals of Jackson County."[52]

The *Journal* continued:

> *She was attired in a cloth dress, which fitted her plump form neatly and a fur-trimmed dolman of black brocaded velvet. Her blonde hair was fluffed and frizzled over her forehead. A diminutive piece of headgear, surmounted by ostrich tips and an orange-colored feather, was held in place by ribbons that were tied beneath her rotund chin.*

The *Journal*'s recounting of Alice's history was even less flattering than its description of her physical appearance. The paper said that Alice, who was orphaned as a child, had been friendly, good-looking, and respected during her girlhood, but she'd gotten into trouble when she was fourteen and "entered upon a wayward life.…Her descent was rapid, and it was not long before she became the associate of the vilest and most desperate characters of both sexes in the city." Alice had a long history of encounters with police. She had degraded not only herself but also those with whom she associated. No fewer than four men, two white and two Black, with whom she had lived at one time or another had been sent to the penitentiary for thievery committed at her instigation. For two years, she had presided over a house of ill fame on East Levee Street that was the "headquarters of a gang of as tough criminals as ever occupied a felon's cell." Afterward, she had gone to Leavenworth and had come back to Kansas City just a few weeks prior to her shooting of John Hamilton.[53]

The only witness called on the first day of testimony was John Wright, who basically repeated what he and Fristoe had told the police on the night of the incident and what Fristoe had said at the coroner's inquest. Wright swore that he and his companions had not been to Alice Dyke's place prior to the shooting and that Hamilton did not try to break down the door, as the defense asserted.[54]

Among the witnesses who testified the next day, October 21, was Officer Williams Burns, who arrived at the Dyke residence with the patrol wagon. He said that when he asked who did the shooting, Alice Dyke denied that she had done it. She also stated that there was no gun in her house, but a pistol was later found on a windowsill in the house. In addition, another officer testified that the two young girls who lived with Alice Dyke told him that Alice had done the shooting.[55]

After the second officer, the final prosecution witness, completed his testimony, Judge Henry White announced that he was inclined to instruct the jury to find the defendant guilty of murder in the second degree because he felt that she might have had just cause in feeling threatened by the words and actions of the deceased. The prosecutor jumped up in protest, proclaiming that Alice was "a common prostitute" and that all the evidence thus far had shown that the killing had been done "in cold blood." Judge White then agreed to withhold his decision, and the defense began presenting its side of the story.[56]

A night watchman named Andrew Pratt testified that he saw three men kicking at Alice Dyke's door around midnight on July 30. He then heard a female voice, followed by the sound of the door opening and a gun firing. A man who worked across the street from the Dyke house backed up Pratt's testimony, as did a woman who lived next door to Alice. The owner of the house Alice lived in then took the stand and testified that when she visited the house on Sunday, July 31, she noticed marks on the front door that had not been there when she had visited the previous day. She thought they looked as if someone had been kicking the door.[57]

Testifying in her own defense, Alice said Hamilton, Fristoe, and Wright were in the front room of her house, which served as a cigar store, about nine o'clock on Saturday night. Hamilton bought a bottle of pop from Minnie Hall and objected to the ten-cent price. Fristoe, whom Alice knew because he'd been to her place before and had caused disturbances, advised Hamilton not to pay the ten cents, but Hamilton tossed a dime down as the three men started out. At the door, Fristoe paused and told Minnie and Alice that he and his companions would get even before the night was over—that they would come back and "tear the damn house down."[58]

Alice said she locked up before midnight, which was earlier than normal, in hopes of discouraging the three men from coming back. Shortly after midnight, however, as she was counting her money in a back room, she heard someone pounding and kicking at the front door. She dimmed the lights in the room in the hope that whoever it was would take the hint and leave, but instead the men started cursing her, calling her names, and demanding that she open the door or else they'd break it down. Retreating to the interior of the house, she got a pistol from Minnie. Starting back toward the front, she heard the sound of shattering glass as a rock crashed through the window of the door. Then, when she got to the door, it flew open and hit her in the chest. Hamilton stood there in the open doorway, and she leveled the pistol at him and fired.[59]

During the state's rebuttal, the prosecutor focused much of his effort on attacking Alice's reputation. An ex-police captain testified, for instance, that he'd known Alice about eight years and that her reputation was bad. The prosecutor attempted to elicit testimony from the captain that Alice had been "the mistress of negro men and that she associated with criminals," but Judge White disallowed such a line of questioning. On cross-examination, the captain was forced to admit that, despite Alice's immoral reputation, he had always found her to be truthful.[60]

Another police officer confirmed that Alice was "a bearer of a bad reputation," and a couple of different witnesses testified that, when they examined the front door to Alice's house after the shooting, they saw no evidence that it had been broken or damaged badly enough to suggest that it had been forced open. W.W. Fristoe was recalled to deny that he and his companions had been in Alice's house around nine o'clock on Saturday evening.[61]

After arguments ended on Saturday, October 22, Judge White gave instructions for verdicts ranging from first-degree murder to acquittal, and the jury retired to deliberate. Unable to reach a quick verdict, the jury deliberated throughout the weekend before coming back on Monday morning with a verdict finding Alice guilty of murder in the second degree and assessing punishment at fifteen years in prison. Newspapers reported that most of the jurors thought Alice was guilty of first-degree murder and should hang for the crime, but two or three held out for acquittal or for a lower degree of guilt. The second-degree verdict represented a compromise between the divergent views.[62]

Alice showed little emotion when the verdict was read. Her attorneys announced almost immediately that they would appeal the decision, and they made good on the promise three days later when they filed a motion for a new trial, citing several judicial errors during the proceedings. When the petition was denied in early December, the defense lawyers announced their attention to file a motion for an arrest in judgment and, if necessary, to appeal to the Missouri Supreme Court. They asked for a delay in sentencing until they could perfect the appeal. In mid-December, Judge White denied the motion for an arrest in judgment and formally pronounced sentence. However, he granted a stay in execution so the defense could prepare its appeal.[63]

When the defense still had not perfected its appeal over a month later, the stay was lifted, and the blue-eyed, fair-complected Alice was transported to the state penitentiary at Jefferson City in early February 1888. Her lack of a religious preference, her bad "habits of life," and her ability to read and write were noted in the prison register.[64]

In late November 1888, the Missouri high court reversed Alice's conviction and remanded her case to Jackson County for retrial. The justices ruled that the trial judge had erred in not granting Alice's request for a continuance based on the absence of an important defense witness. The ruling was met with public outrage. The *Kansas City Times*, for instance, reminded its readers of the "cold-blooded" nature of Alice's crime. The prosecutor in her case said he didn't think the supposed absent witness even existed.[65]

A newspaper reporter interviewed Alice briefly after she was brought back to Kansas City and lodged in the Second Street Jail. Alice said that she'd been employed as an assistant turnkey in the female division of the penitentiary in Jefferson City and that she had no complaint about the treatment she'd received there, although she was glad to be back in Kansas City. The reporter who interviewed her opined that Alice would probably never be convicted again, as the witnesses against her were scattered here and there and one important witness had recently died.[66]

In response to the public criticism of the supreme court's decision, Alice's lawyer clarified that the decision was based on more than just Judge White's failure to grant a continuance. For instance, White had also erred in allowing testimony about the character of the house and the neighborhood where the crime was committed.[67]

In mid-January 1889, when Alice's new trial was set to begin, Judge White, who'd denied Alice's request for a continuance, granted one to the state because W.W. Fristoe was somewhere in Texas and could not be reached at this time. Alice's attorneys objected on the grounds that Fristoe's testimony was essentially the same as John Wright's and Wright was present.[68]

When Alice's retrial came up in April 1889, the testimony for both sides was generally consistent with what had been presented at her first trial. However, according to at least one observer, the state did not put forward "as strong a case against the accused as on the previous trial," and an acquittal or a light sentence was expected. Prior to jury deliberation, Judge White gave instructions for verdicts of murder in the second degree and for not guilty by reason of self-defense. After the jury had been out several days, longer than any jury in Jackson County history, they came back and told White they were hopelessly deadlocked, and he declared a mistrial. Alice, whose conduct had been good during her imprisonment, was released on bond to appear at her next trial.[69]

When Alice's third trial got underway in September 1889, the state's case was "very weak," owing to the absence of at least two critical witnesses. In addition, the testimony of one of the main witnesses who did appear for the state, John Wright, was called into question when several witnesses for the defense testified that his reputation for truthfulness was bad. On the evening of September 16, the jury came back with a not guilty verdict after three or four hours of deliberation. On the first ballot, the vote stood ten in favor of acquittal and two in favor of a second-degree murder conviction, and it took eleven more ballots before all twelve jurors finally agreed. After the not-guilty verdict was announced, Alice sobbed, thanked and shook hands with the jurors, and was then ushered from the courtroom by some of her friends.[70]

In July 1890, Alice was arrested during a raid on a "disreputable house" in Kansas City, but she produced a marriage certificate showing that, under the name Nellie Kelly, she had recently married Sam Halley, the man who was staying with her at the house. She explained that Nellie Kelly was her real name and that Alice Dyke was an assumed name. Nellie, a.k.a. Alice, was then discharged.[71]

4

"KILL THE SON OF A BITCH"

THE STORY OF BLANCHE CONNORS

In the wee hours of Sunday, December 25, 1887, the body of a man identified as Joseph Peters, "a colored hod-carrier," was found in Kansas City in a pool of blood near the intersection of Ninth Street and State Line Road on the Missouri side of the line. Peters had two deep cuts in his groin, one of which had severed an artery.[72]

Shortly after daylight on Christmas morning, Sergeant T.S. Boulware, a police officer assigned to the case, followed a trail of blood along Ninth Street to Genessee Street and north on Genessee to where he discovered another pool of blood in front of the home of Jane "Aunt Jane" Grisby. On inquiry, Boulware learned that Aunt Jane had hosted a Christmas Eve party on Saturday night at which "bad whiskey flowed freely" and that there had been a serious disturbance at the party.[73]

About one o'clock in the morning, an "octoroon named Blanche Connors" was playing the organ when Peters stepped up to her and whispered something in her ear. Almost instantly, a Black man named Paul Enders struck Peters and the two ran out of the house, followed by Blanche and a third man, later identified as George Thomas, alias Bony George. Boulware found Enders and the woman at a house near the corner of Eight and Hickory Streets, where they lived. Enders was in bed, and a knife that appeared to have been recently washed lay on the bed. Blanche was wearing an apron that had blood on it and had a cut in it.[74]

Blanche and Enders said they knew nothing of the murder and claimed not even to know Peters. Blanche said she remembered several men running out of the house at one point during the party and creating a noise outside, but she was drunk at the time and didn't think much about the incident. She didn't know whether Enders was one of the men or not. Explaining the cut in her apron, she said that a man with a knife in his hand had pushed her while they were inside the house and that she must have gotten the cut at that time. Despite their protests of innocence, Boulware placed both suspects under arrest.[75]

A coroner's inquest was held over Peters's body a day or two after his death. The most important witness was a young Black woman named Alice Marr. She had witnessed the killing, and she said Paul Enders, Bony George, and Blanche Conners (alias Matt or Mattie Mason) had the victim down in the yard in front of Aunt Jane's house. She heard Blanche say, "Kill the son of a bitch," and George replied, "I have cut him and have got his money." Peters got up and started staggering toward Ninth Street, but George went after him and knocked him down again. Then, Blanche, Bony George, and Enders left in a hurry. Alice said she saw Enders the next morning and asked him why they were beating that man last night. He told her they'd attacked Peters because they wanted his money, that "the damned son of a bitch" was dead, and that he didn't care. Enders said he and Mattie each got twenty-five dollars that they'd taken from the murdered man. Enders told Alice not to tell on them and that he'd give her part of the money, but she told him she didn't want any of it. Two or three other witnesses gave testimony that tended to corroborate Alice's, although they had not actually seen the cutting.[76]

When the inquest ended on December 28, the coroner's jury ruled that Joseph Peters had come to his death by wounds inflicted with a knife by either Paul Enders, Bony George Thomas, or Blanche Connors and that, regardless of which one had inflicted the fatal wound, the other two were active accomplices. The next morning, Enders and Blanche were arrested and charged with murder, but Thomas could not be located.[77]

Enders's case was severed from Blanche's, and he was tried first, in February 1888. The jury failed to agree, in large part, no doubt, because Alice Marr, the state's star witness, had disappeared, and the judge declared a mistrial.[78]

Blanche's case was continued to allow the state time to track down Marr and another missing witness. When Blanche's trial began in mid-April, she sat in the courtroom "gorgeously arrayed," according to the *Kansas City Star*, "watching with evident interest the selection of the special jury." The rival *Kansas City Journal* described her at the time as "a good-looking octoroon, about 25 years of age." The *Journal* thought the state could make a stronger case against Blanche than the one they'd presented against Paul Enders because Blanche was said to have instigated the crime.[79]

The evidence against Blanche was similar to that presented at Enders's trial, but the state did, indeed, build a stronger circumstantial case against her than it had against Enders. Although Alice Marr was again absent, several other witnesses gave damning testimony. The most important proved to be Willie Sells, a thirteen-year-old boy who was at Aunt Jane's house on the night of the crime. He said he'd been in the same room with Blanche and Joe Peters, had seen them talking to each other for several minutes, and had heard Blanche call Peters a vile name. When Peters got up to leave the room, Blanche tried to block his way, but he got through the door and walked out of the house. Willie then saw Blanche whisper something to Bony George Thomas. Thomas followed Peters out of the house, and Blanche followed Thomas. Willie's dog followed them, and Willie followed the dog out to the gate. He saw Blanche and two men fighting, with Blanche and one of the men standing over the other man. To avoid getting drawn into the trouble, he then turned and went back inside. The only weakness in Willie's testimony was that he did not account for Paul Enders's alleged involvement in the crime. Another boy, a fifteen-year-old grandson of Aunt Jane, said he'd seen Enders and Bony George shortly after five thirty on Christmas morning scraping snow to try to cover up the blood in front of his grandmother's house.[80]

Before the jury retired to deliberate, Judge Henry White, the same judge who'd tried Alice Dyke's case, instructed the jury to return either a verdict of first-degree murder or an acquittal, because there was no evidence the killing had been committed in the heat of the moment as a crime of passion. On April 23, the jury, after being out forty-eight hours, came back with a verdict of first-degree murder. Blanche Connors thus became the first woman in Jackson County ever convicted of first-degree murder. The jury's first ballot was said to have stood seven to five in favor of conviction, but an examination of the apron Blanche wore on the night of the crime led several jurymen to change their vote. Blanche received the verdict with reported indifference and refused at first to talk to anyone.[81]

A short time later, however, she was interviewed by a *Kansas City Times* reporter, who described her as "a handsome quadroon" with "great brown eyes." The "quadroon" appellation was accurate, even though the term would be considered politically incorrect today, because Blanche was, in fact, one-fourth Black, not one-eighth as "octaroon," the term by which she'd been

Blanche Connors, as sketched by rival newspapers at the time of her trial. *From the Kansas City Times (left) and the Kansas City Journal (right).*

described in previous reports, denotes. The *Times* reporter also learned that Blanche was only twenty years old, not in her mid-twenties as previously estimated. She would not turn twenty-one for another two or three months, she said, and her last name was Connor, not Connors, as it had been routinely spelled in newspapers.[82]

Blanche's maiden name was Martha "Mattie" Mason, and she had been born in the Indian Nation, the daughter of a full-blooded Cherokee mother and a half-Black, half-Cherokee father. Her mother died when she was only eight days old, and when she was four years old, she was taken to Iowa, where she lived and associated mainly with Black people, owing to her father's Black ancestry. When she was six, she was taken to Franklin County, Missouri, where a German woman took her in to raise. Blanche said she had not seen her father since she was eight years old. She was still a mere girl when she struck out on her own and moved to St. Louis. She married a Black man named George Connor when she was seventeen, but they stayed together only about a year. She got the nickname Blanche because of her light complexion.[83]

According to the *Times*, since Blanche had been in the Second Street Jail, she had been "one of the most quiet and best behaved of all the prisoners." Blanche said she was surprised by her first-degree murder conviction, because all the evidence presented against her was circumstantial. She said the apron that was used as a crucial bit of evidence against her was not hers at all. Instead, it belonged to Adeline Murray, Aunt Jane Grigsby's daughter, but Adeline had come to the place where Blanche was staying not long after the trouble at Aunt Jane's house and asked if Blanche would trade aprons with her because hers (Adeline's) was dirty. Blanche agreed and tossed the dirty apron on a shelf, where Officer Boulware found it the next morning.[84]

When the reporter mentioned Bony George, Blanche spoke bitterly about him, claiming she didn't like him and never had anything to do with him because, eight years earlier, he had married a cousin of Blanche's and treated her very badly. Blanche's cousin had been dead for some time, and Bony George was now Adeline Murray's man and had been for a long time. Blanche questioned why authorities had been unable to find Bony George, since it was known that he had been in and around St. Louis and Chicago and had been sending money and packages to Adeline.[85]

Blanche finished the interview by declaring that she was an innocent girl, but she said if she had to hang or go to prison, she wouldn't be the first innocent person to suffer. If she had to do likewise, she guessed there was nothing to do but accept her fate, but she hoped she would "come out right in the end."[86]

A couple of days after her conviction, Blanche's attorneys filed a motion for a new trial. Among the grounds for the motion was the contention that the jury should not have been allowed to examine the torn and bloody apron during deliberations without the presence or the consent of the defense.[87]

Prison life seemed not to dampen Blanche's spirits. Over two months after her conviction, while Judge White awaited developments in the Enders case before ruling on Blanche's motion or passing sentence on her, the *Kansas City Star* observed that Blanche was "one of the most jovial prisoners in the Second Street Jail."[88]

Thursday was visitors' day at the jail, and according to the *Star*, the inmates looked forward to the day with anticipation. They would get up early, attend to their toilet, and be ready to greet the line of visitors, including strangers, who called at the jail. Nearly all the visitors wanted to see Blanche, and she very much enjoyed their visit. The *Star* reporter continued:

> *She very early in the day arrays herself in her brightest ribbons and, seated on a chair, waits for the public inspection. She readily enters into conversation with the white visitors but does not deign to converse with the colored people. The fact of her conviction does not seem to rest heavily upon her mind, for she expresses her opinion emphatically that she will never be hanged.*

The reporter agreed that Blanche's pretty neck would likely "never have a noose adjusted about it."[89]

At Paul Enders's second trial in late January 1889, key witnesses, including Alice Marr, were again missing. After contentious arguments, in which each side accused the other of paying witnesses to disappear or to give false testimony, the jury got the case on the night of January 30 and came back the next afternoon with a verdict of not guilty. A month later, Judge White granted Blanche's motion for a new trial. Speaking directly to Blanche, he told her that her conviction had been based almost solely on the testimony of Willie Sells, that enough had happened since then to call his testimony into question, and that she, therefore, deserved a second chance.[90]

At Blanche's second trial in April 1889, the state's case again suffered from the absence of important witnesses, and the only choice Judge White gave the jury was between first-degree murder and acquittal. The panel stood three for conviction and nine for acquittal on the first ten ballots, but the holdouts for conviction changed their votes to not guilty on the eleventh ballot. When the verdict was announced, Blanche seemed dazed, and she slumped to her chair and wept. After her discharge, she reportedly left the courthouse in the company of a Black woman who kept a bawdy house on Broadway.[91]

On June 2, 1890, Blanche was heard from again. About noon on that day, she and two other women were drinking beer at a questionable resort at 606 West Fifth Street in Kansas City when Blanche and one of the other women, Ida Whiteside, got into an argument. Whiteside ran into her room to get a gun, but before she could retrieve the weapon, Blanche shot her twice with .32-caliber revolver. Whiteside was not gravely wounded, but Blanche was charged with assault with intent to kill and released on bond. She was convicted in December 1890 and sentenced to two years in the state penitentiary. She was discharged in June 1892 on the three-fourths rule, which allowed for early release for good behavior. What happened to Blanche after that has not been traced.[92]

5

"I HAVE KILLED PETE"

MAUD LEWIS MURDERS HER LOVER

About two forty-five in the morning on Monday, May 13, 1895, policemen Dave Moore and George Donnelly, who were patrolling the vicinity of Elliott Avenue and Wash Street (now Cole Street) in St. Louis, heard two shots ring out. At first, they couldn't locate where the sound had come from, but a young woman named Lillian Moss almost immediately rushed up to them and announced that Maud Lewis, madam of the house where Lillian boarded at 2719 Wash Street, had just shot Missouri State Senator Pete Morrissey.[93]

The officers hurried to the designated house and found it in pandemonium. They got there in time to intercept Albert Andrews, porter at the Lewis house, as he was trying to leave, but he was highly excited and unable to give them an intelligent account of what had happened. They found Morrissey's dead body lying in Maud's bed with "a ragged red hole" where his right eye had been and blood and brains oozing out of the hole. His mouth was also "a mass of mangled flesh and clotted blood." Maud Lewis, twenty-eight, was in a hysteric state bordering on insanity. Two professional men who had accompanied Senator Morrissey to the questionable resort, Dr. Charles Frank and Dr. Thomas O'Reilly, were "very much worried over the terrible affair." Lillian Moss and her housemate Ella Lewis, who had been entertaining the doctors, seemed to know almost nothing about the matter except that they'd heard the shots.[94]

Assistant St. Louis Police Chief Patrick Reedy arrived within minutes to take charge of the investigation, and he began interviewing the occupants of the home.

Dr. Frank said that he and O'Reilly had been at Senator Morrissey's saloon on the corner of Eleventh Street and Clark Avenue about midnight on Sunday night talking and drinking with Morrissey when Maud Lewis, who was generally known as the senator's "mistress," came in, accompanied by Lillian Moss, and joined the three men. After the women had been there an hour or two, Maud started trying to get Morrissey to go back to her place with him. He didn't want to at first, but he finally agreed and asked the doctors to go with him. After some hesitation, they, too, consented to go to Maud's place, and the drunken entourage of five repaired to her house. It was about two thirty on Monday morning or shortly afterward when they got there.[95]

Senator Morrissey went into Maud's room with her, and the two doctors went upstairs with Lillian and Ella. Dr. Frank said that not more than ten to fifteen minutes later he and the others heard two gunshots downstairs. The gunfire was followed immediately by Maud's voice, screaming that Pete was dead. The occupants of the house disagreed on whether she said, "They have killed Pete," or "I have killed Pete." When those who had been upstairs reached Maud's room, she was standing, half-dressed, beside the bed, where Morrissey lay dead.[96]

Albert Andrews, the porter, told Chief Reedy that, a few minutes before the shooting, he heard Maud say, "Don't, Pete. Don't." However, he couldn't tell whether she was angry. When he heard the shots, he ran to the stairs and saw a man going out the front door. Andrews then rushed down the stairs to Maud's room and saw Morrissey lying dead and a .38-caliber revolver on the bed beside him. Andrews picked the weapon up and put it in his pocket, where police later found it and took it from him. Further investigation revealed that the revolver was almost certainly the murder weapon, that it belonged to Morrissey, and that he'd placed it on the nightstand when he entered Maud's room. Neither the doctors nor the young women in the house had seen any such stranger as the man Andrews claimed to have seen fleeing the house, and police were inclined to believe the man was a figment of the porter's imagination. This impression was reinforced a few days later when it was revealed that Andrews was a morphine addict with a history of run-ins with the law.[97]

After interviewing the occupants of the Lewis house, Chief Reedy ordered Maud's arrest. "She resisted violently, and being a large and extremely muscular woman, it required the efforts of several officers to handle her." Because she was so hysterical, she was sent to the city hospital and "chained to a cot."[98]

Left: Sketch of Maud Lewis at the time of her arrest. *From the St. Louis Post-Dispatch.*

Right: Sketch of Peter Morrissey, Maud's victim. *From the St. Louis Globe-Democrat.*

At an inquest held over Morrissey's body on Monday afternoon, the coroner's jury reached a verdict that the senator had come to his death from gunshots fired from a pistol by "one Maud Lewis." Some doubt was expressed concerning the woman's sanity, based not just on her hysterical behavior since the shooting but also on her history. A year or so earlier, Maud had been a patient in the city hospital, and at that time her mind was said to have been affected by a blow to her head that Morrissey had delivered.[99]

On Monday evening, about the time of the inquest or shortly afterward, a *St. Louis Globe-Democrat* reporter visited Maud in her cell at the Four Courts Jail. She was "very nervous…had a wild look in her eyes," and was reluctant to talk when the reporter first called on her, but later she calmed down and gradually opened up. She admitted that her real name was Fay O'Neil, not Maud Lewis, but she declined to go into further detail about her personal background. The next day, she told another newspaper that Fay O'Neil was just a cover and that her real maiden name was Laura Lucas.[100]

Maud's story of the events leading up to Morrissey's death differed little from that of Dr. Frank, except that, whereas Frank had mentioned only an argument at the saloon, Maud stressed that Morrissey had mistreated and physically abused her. In fact, she said, he had treated her roughly ever since they'd known each other, but she still loved him and wasn't jealous, even though she suspected he had other girlfriends. The only thing she resented was that she had sacrificed for him, tried to do right by him, and even given him money, and he repaid her by mistreating her. As for the killing itself, Maud admitted that she must have done it, but she didn't know exactly how it happened and didn't even remember pulling the trigger. She said that both she and Morrissey had been drinking heavily leading up to the incident.[101]

A few days after the shooting, Maud was charged with first-degree murder. When her preliminary hearing was called in late May, Dr. Frank gave a statement similar to what he'd told Chief Reedy, except he added that, when he heard the gunshots and hurried down to the defendant's room, he saw her and Albert Andrews struggling over the revolver. Maud said she wanted the revolver because she'd killed Pete and wanted to kill herself. After Frank's testimony, the proceeding was continued.[102]

Albert Andrews's apparent attempt to shield Maud by telling the story about seeing a stranger run from her house prompted rumors that there might be more to their relationship than met the public eye. Andrews's history of encounters with police and Maud's reluctance to talk about her own past added fuel to the speculation, and a *St. Louis Post-Dispatch* reporter resolved to investigate both of their backgrounds. Delving into court records, he found that Maud, under the name of Laura Andrews or Mrs. A.A. Andrews, had been arrested in St. Louis thirteen years earlier for stealing a dog, and the case had been bitterly fought in court. Her husband, Albert A. Andrews, had appeared as a witness in the case. Confronted with these facts, Maud denied that she and Andrews were ever legally married. She admitted they'd had a common-law bond at one time, but even that relationship, she said, was shattered long ago. She now considered him just a friend and an employee. She claimed that the only ties that bound them, according to the reporter, were "those of an indulgent mistress and the pitiable hireling who clung" to her "like the leech to the artery from which it sucks its sustenance."[103]

When Maud's preliminary hearing concluded in mid-June, the defense offered a plea of self-defense. Testifying on her own behalf, Maud said that she and Morrissey had argued in her room prior to the shooting, that he had beat and choked her, but that she didn't remember what happened after that. Despite Maud's teary-eyed testimony, the judge ruled that she should stand trial for second-degree murder, and she was returned to jail in lieu of $5,000 bond.[104]

On July 23, a *St. Louis Post-Dispatch* reporter visited Maud in her cell at the Four Courts and found her more pleasant and communicative than she'd been when first brought into the jail over two months earlier. Not only had her temperament improved, but so, too, had her appearance. When first arrested, Maud was an "unkempt, bloated and slovenly-clad creature," but now her eyes were bright, her hair "becomingly arranged," and her clothes "neat-fitting." Despite her life of dissipation, the reporter said, she still "showed traces of having been a handsome woman," and her manner and intelligence suggested that she'd been reared in "surroundings totally different from those amidst which she was found on the morning of the murder."[105]

Prompted to talk about her past, Maud told the newspaperman that she didn't know why his readers would be interested in her life because it had been "prosaic enough to suit anyone." She admitted, however, that she found "a certain amount of relief in living over in my mind the old days before I knew the meaning of sin."[106]

Falling back on the story she'd told just after her arrest, Maud said her father's name was James O'Neil, that he was a cotton merchant in New Orleans, and that her given name was Fayette. Her mother was an educated woman who taught Maud at home until she was nine years old, at which time she'd been placed in a convent in New Orleans. Her father died when she was about twelve, and her mother soon passed away as well. She was then adopted by a childless couple named Scott, who raised Maud as their own child. The man was a grocer who had been a friend of Maud's father. She lived with the couple until she was sixteen, when she met a thirty-year-old man named Harry Spencer at a party, became infatuated with him, and married him hastily.[107]

Spencer was a traveling salesman who was often on the road, and Maud usually accompanied him wherever he went. She enjoyed the nomadic life at first but soon realized that she no longer loved Spencer because she was "full of life and gaiety," while he was "all business." He was tired at the end of each day and didn't want to do anything, while she was eager to go out and have fun. The couple spent a good deal of time in St. Louis, and on one of their sojourns there in the summer of 1890, Maud met Peter Morrissey and was "struck with him from the moment we were introduced."[108]

Morrissey knew Maud was married, but he seemed enamored of her, too, and they started seeing each other secretly. When Spencer prepared to leave on a business trip, Maud begged him to let her stay in St. Louis. He reluctantly agreed, as long as she stayed with some of their mutual friends, but she spent much of her time with Morrissey. When Spencer returned, he heard rumors about Maud and Morrissey, and he took her to task about the gossip. She vigorously denied the rumors and continued to see Morrissey, but when Spencer finally confronted her with evidence of her infidelity, she broke down and admitted the affair. She told Spencer she no longer loved him but loved Morrissey instead. More hurt than angry, Spencer packed up his things and left, and Maud never saw him again.[109]

Abandoned and without means, even though her destitute situation was her "own fault," Maud made up her mind to act at once. She went out of the hotel where she and Spencer had been staying and asked a cabman to drive her to "an immoral resort." The next day, when she told Morrissey what she'd done, he was angry at first but finally let her stay at the dubious resort until he could find and furnish her with a place of her own. She ended up staying for seven months at the questionable retreat, where she learned to drink and drown her troubles in liquor. Morrissey continued to call on her during this time, and at the end the seven months, he kept his promise and put her up in place near downtown St. Louis, where he visited her three or four times a week. Maud said she knew Morrissey sometimes saw other women, and they often argued about that and other matters, especially when he was drunk, but they "always made up the next day and loved each other even more."[110]

Maud stayed in the place downtown until about the first of the year in 1894, when Morrissey moved her to a different house, the one where he died. Maud now claimed that she had not killed Morrissey and didn't know who did. If she had confessed to the killing, as she'd been told was the case, she must have been crazy to have made such a confession. Without even considering her deep love for Morrissey, why, she asked, would she be foolish enough to kill him when she stood to lose all the good things he had showered on her? At this point, Maud broke down and started crying, announced that she'd already told the reporter more than she should have, and got up and walked away toward her cell.[111]

There was just one thing wrong with Maud's elaborate story. Most of it was a lie. Perhaps she'd forgotten that she'd previously admitted that her name was not Fay O'Neil but rather Laura Lucas and that the O'Neil yarn was just a cover story. In fact, the *St. Louis Post-Dispatch* itself had previously discredited her claim to be the daughter of cotton merchant James O'Neil. She was instead the daughter of an old riverman named Dan Lucas, who allegedly had once shot several Black men in order to quell a riot on his boat. Maud's story might have had elements of truth. For instance, she might have been romantically involved with a man named Harry Spencer at one time, but there's no record that she was ever legally married to such a man. There's no such doubt about her marriage to Albert Andrews, though. She legally wed him in St. Louis in 1880. In addition, Maud, or Laura, was about four years older than she claimed to be when she was arrested.[112]

In mid-August, Albert Andrews signed a written confession that he, not Maud, had killed Pete Morrissey. He claimed to have done so after he saw Morrissey knock Maud down, and he said the reason Maud remembered nothing about the actual killing was that she was unconscious at the time. In speaking to reporters after his confession, Andrews gave the impression that, even though Morrissey had broken up his once-happy home, he had not acted out of anger toward the senator but out of concern for Maud's welfare. Although the confession was convincing in its detail, not everyone believed Andrews's story. The police, for instance, felt he was just trying to protect his estranged wife. Despite the skepticism, Andrews was shortly afterward arrested on the basis of his confession and charged with murder.[113]

In reporting the confession, the *St. Louis Globe-Democrat* upbraided Maud for her persistence in lying about her relationship to Andrews and about her own background. The newspaper could only conjecture that her motive for doing so was an attempt to shield her family and the man she had once loved (i.e. Andrews) from the disgrace that she had brought upon herself.[114]

At Maud's trial in October 1895, Dr. O'Reilly testified that he saw Andrews coming down the stairs almost immediately after the shots that killed Morrissey were fired and that Andrews, therefore, could not have been the one who fired the shots. The state also sought to show that the shooting did not occur during a struggle but while Morrissey was lying defenseless on the bed. Maud's attorney, on the other hand, argued that Andrews did, indeed, shoot Morrissey and even if Maud shot him, she did so in an act of self-defense or temporary insanity brought on by Morrissey's habitual abuse of her.[115]

The jury got the case on the evening of October 18 and came back the next morning with a verdict finding Maud guilty of second-degree murder and assessing punishment at fifteen years in prison. After the verdict was announced, Andrews reportedly retracted his confession, admitting that he'd given it only in an attempt to save Maud.[116]

Despite the verdict against Maud, there was considerable sentiment in her favor. Senator Morrissey had been thrice indicted for fraud, had a reputation for debauchery, and was known to abuse Maud with regularity. So, there were many people who were "not prone to judge too harshly her who cut him short in his career."[117]

Maud was released on $4,000 bond pending a ruling on her motion for a new trial. When she arrived at her a sister's house on Warren Street in St. Louis to take up temporary residence there, neighbors of the sister, expecting to see the woman they had known as Laura Lucas, were surprised to see instead Maud Lewis, the notorious murderess, and to realize that the two women were one and the same. The neighbors felt Maud should not be allowed to abide among "respectable people," and the sister's landlady began proceedings to have her evicted.[118]

In early January 1896, Maud's motion for a new trial was denied. Her lawyer then appealed to the Missouri Supreme Court, and she remained free on bond. On November 20 of the same year, the high court affirmed Maud's conviction, and she was transported to the state penitentiary at Jefferson City the next day.[119]

Within a few months after Maud's imprisonment, some of her friends and relatives began petitioning for clemency in her case. Since Maud's conviction, Andrews had once again signed a written confession that he and not Maud had killed Morrissey, and additional evidence of Morrissey's abuse of Maud had also been uncovered. So, not only did considerable doubt exist as to Maud's guilt, said the petitioners, but also, if she did kill the senator, she was wholly justified in doing so. In addition, Maud was in frail health. After resisting pleas on Maud's behalf for a couple of years, Governor Lon Stephens finally pardoned her in early January 1901 on the condition that she leave the state of Missouri and that her sister, who had promised to see to Maud's care, follow up on that promise. Maud was discharged after serving a little over four years of her fifteen-year term.[120]

6
A SHOTGUN WEDDING TURNS DEADLY
THE STORY OF LULU PRINCE

When thirty-year-old Phillip H. Kennedy and twenty-two-year-old Lulu Prince were married on December 4, 1900, at the courthouse in Kansas City, the local *Times* thought the ceremony was "a queer wedding," to say the least. There were "no flowers, no music, and no bridesmaids," and both the bride's father and older brother Will, who were the only other members of the wedding party, seemed angry. While the marriage license was being issued in the recorder's office, the father and his prospective son-in-law exchanged heated words.[121]

None of the wedding party wanted to discuss the imminent marriage with a *Times* courthouse reporter who was on the scene. Kennedy, who seemed nervous and excited, beseeched the reporter not even mention the marriage, but Lulu, in response, urged the newspaperman to "go ahead and publish it. I want it published," she said. "I have excellent reasons for it."[122]

Judge James Gibson performed the ceremony in his chamber, and after he admonished the couple, prior to the exchange of vows, about the sacred obligation existing between a man and a woman who entered into holy matrimony, Kennedy "curled his lip and heaved a sigh that could be heard half a block away." He "did not take his bride by the hand while the solemn words were being spoken" but, on the contrary, "stood with his arms crossed and gazed at the ceiling." He declined to kiss the bride when the ceremony was over and, instead, made a dash for the door.[123]

Lulu's father, C.W. Prince, halted Kennedy with a command for him to come back and pay the judge for performing the marriage. Kennedy reluctantly obliged and then "made a beeline for the elevator, his bride almost running to keep up with him. He went down stairs and rushed from the building, the other members of the wedding party trailing after him."[124]

Quoting a courthouse lounger, the *Times* reporter summed up the strange matrimonial scene as "a 'rush affair' from beginning to end."[125]

Barely over a month later, the curious story of the Kennedy marriage made headlines again, when the groom applied to the circuit court on January 8, 1901, to annul, in the words of the *Kansas City Times*, "one of the strangest marriage contracts ever entered into in Jackson County." The couple had "never established a home or spent a single hour together" since the wedding ceremony, and Kennedy alleged in his petition that he'd entered into the marriage under duress and never would have married Lulu of his own free will. He refused further comment about the matter to a *Times* reporter, except to say that he was "up against it" and wanted "the unpleasant affair settled." He added that he married the girl only because his life was threatened.[126]

Kennedy also refused to talk about the relationship between him and Lulu prior to their wedding or the circumstances that led to such a hasty ceremony.[127]

The hurry-up Kennedy wedding had caused a minor stir when the ceremony was performed back in December, and now it set the whole town on its ear, with all three of Kansas City's major newspapers carrying stories about the groom's petition to annul the month-old marriage. Readers could hardly have predicted that the case was about to take an even more sensational turn.

On the night after the December 4 wedding, Kennedy had called on Lulu at her father's house and taken her to the theater, but he refused to live with her and, in fact, let it be known that he wanted nothing more to do with her. On Saturday, December 8, Lulu met with a *Kansas City Star* reporter and tried to get him to write another story clarifying the reason for her hasty marriage. She said the previous stories had left the impression that Kennedy was forced to marry her because of "their intimate relations," and she said that was not true. The real reason was simply that she and Kennedy had been engaged, and when she found out that he was planning to wed another young woman, she was determined to hold him to his promise of marriage. The reporter subsequently contacted Kennedy, who denied that he had ever been engaged to Lulu Prince.[128]

In early January 1901, C.W. Prince visited Kennedy in his office and demanded forty dollars in compensation for his daughter's board and maintenance since her marriage to Kennedy. The men exchanged heated words, and Prince called Kennedy a "rape fiend." Lulu also visited or spoke by phone with Kennedy several times after her marriage, trying to get him to change his mind about living with her as a man and wife, including at least one "stormy confrontation" in his office. After Lulu learned from the January 9 Kansas City newspapers that her estranged husband had filed a motion for an annulment the previous day, her hope for a reconciliation faded, but she was determined to try again.[129]

On the afternoon of the ninth, she met a *Kansas City Tim*es reporter and aired her grievances against what she thought had been her mistreatment and a misrepresentation of the facts by the press. She said Kennedy's marriage to her was not forced and that the press's depiction of it in that manner had been defamatory to her character. She even claimed that she and Kennedy had lived together for a week after their marriage. This, of course, was not true, and it calls into question the veracity of some of her other statements. On the evening of the ninth, Lulu visited Kennedy in his office, beseeching him to reconsider, but he again rebuffed her.[130]

Driven to desperation, she resolved the next day to give him one last chance, in the form of an ultimatum. Secreting in the folds of her dress a .32-caliber revolver that belonged to her brother Bert, Lulu went to downtown Kansas City at midafternoon on January 10 and called on Dr. R.O. Cross at his office in the Rialto Building. Cross recognized her as the same "good-looking woman" who'd visited him about eight weeks prior under an assumed name and asked him to "make an investigation." He did so and found that the young lady was in "delicate health." This time, Lulu revealed her true identity, telling Dr. Cross that she was the woman who'd been in the news lately about a so-called forced marriage. When the doctor told her, or she told the doctor, that she was still in the same condition she was at the time of her previous visit, Lulu asked him to please go to her husband and explain to him her "exact condition," because she was sure he'd reconsider his annulment suit once he knew the full truth.[131]

Although reluctant to meddle, Dr. Cross finally agreed to talk to Kennedy, and Lulu left. The doctor telephoned Kennedy and arranged to meet him in the latter's office in the Ridge Building, since Kennedy said he could not take off work. Cross arrived at the door of Kennedy's second-floor office about five thirty in the afternoon, and Kennedy stepped out into the hallway to talk to the doctor. When Cross explained Lulu's "exact condition," Kennedy had very little to say, so Cross turned to leave. As he was walking away, Lulu appeared from an elevator and hurried past the doctor without so

The "strikingly beautiful" Lulu Price Kennedy. *From the Kansas City Star.*

much as a glance in his direction. She strode toward Kennedy, who still lingered outside his doorway, and hollered, "Hold up a minute. I want to talk to you." When Lulu demanded to know what Kennedy was going to do now, he said he was done with her for good and waved his hands as if to dismiss her. Suddenly, she whipped out the revolver and fired round after round at him until it was empty. Kennedy staggered toward his office, slumped to the floor, and lay still.[132]

Thomas Kennedy, who had been visiting his brother in the latter's office, hurried out into the hallway, saw Lulu with the smoking gun, and grabbed hold of her. As he was wresting the weapon from her grasp, a young man whom a witness identified as Bert Prince dashed from a nearby stairway, struck Thomas Kennedy, and fled. A doctor whose office was nearby hurried into the hallway, knelt over Phillip Kennedy, and announced, as he was rising, that the man was dead. Breaking away from Thomas Kennedy, Lulu stepped over to where her husband lay on the floor. "He's dead, is he?" She kicked him in the side of the face. "He'll never seduce another girl."[133]

Pushed aside, Lulu turned to a policeman who had arrived on the scene. "Take me way from here," she said. "I can't stand the sight."[134]

The "strikingly beautiful" young woman was taken to the police station, where she impressed observers with her composure and demeanor. Despite a lengthy interrogation, she did not break down and steadfastly declined to go into details about why she'd killed her husband. "It is safe to say," ventured the *Kansas City Journal*, "there was never before a woman prisoner in a Kansas City prison who carried herself so proudly and so well under circumstances anywhere near similar

Phillip Kennedy, Lulu's husband and victim. *From the Kansas City Star.*

to what she went through." Although the general public knew few of the specifics surrounding Lulu's case, many people on the streets of Kansas City expressed sympathy for any girl who defended her honor against a man who wronged her with a false promise of marriage.[135]

A coroner's inquest into Kennedy's death held on January 12 had to be moved to the criminal courtroom to accommodate the crowd of people who wanted to attend. Many of the spectators were female, but Lulu Prince Kennedy, the accused, was "the prettiest woman in the room."[136]

Among those testifying at the inquest was Will Prince, who admitted that he, not his brother, was the person who struck Thomas Kennedy after the shooting. Will said he grew worried about his sister, came looking for her, and reached the entrance to the Ridge Building just as the shots rang out. Seeing a man roughly handling his sister and thinking it was Phillip Kennedy, Will struck the man before he realized what had happened, and he left hurriedly once he realized the circumstances because he knew he might be suspected of abetting his sister.[137]

Will testified that he did not know Lulu was in "delicate" health until just a few hours before the shooting. Corroborating his son's testimony, C.W. Prince said Lulu had confessed to him in early December that Phillip Kennedy had "ruined" her and was about to marry another young woman, which was the cause of the rushed wedding, but he did not know she was in a delicate condition until the day of the shooting.[138]

Several eyewitnesses or near eyewitnesses described the events at the Ridge Building on the afternoon of January 11. Perhaps the most damning testimony to Lulu's defense was given by Dr. Cross. Not only did he describe the shooting in some detail, but he also testified that, when Lulu had first come to him around the first of November 1900, she had identified herself as the wife of Case Patten, a professional baseball player who'd spent the previous summer in Kansas City as a member of the Kansas City Blues.[139]

At the end of the inquest, the coroner's jury returned a verdict that Phillip Kennedy had met his death from gunshots fired by Lulu Prince Kennedy and that she should be held for trial on a charge of first-degree murder. Just a few minutes after the verdict, Lulu was arraigned on the murder charge and committed to the county jail.[140]

Although Lulu held up well when first arrested, her physical and mental health deteriorated to the point that she was almost "shattered" and bordering on collapse ten days later. She quickly revived, however, and was soon back to impressing observers with her beauty and composure. In mid-February, a grand jury returned an indictment of first-degree murder against her. The

Sketch of Lulu Prince Kennedy in her cell after her arrest. *From the Kansas City Times.*

prosecutor had her father and her brother Will arrested as accessories later the same day. An arrest order was also issued for her brother Bert, a professional mandolin player. He was away on a concert tour, but he, too, was arrested a few days later.[141]

Bert Prince, who was considered less culpable in the crime than his father and brother, was released on bond in early March 1901. Friends of the father finally came up with his bond in late March, but Will Prince remained in jail in lieu of $5,000 bond.[142]

Interviewed at the county jail by a *Kansas City Times* reporter on June 2, Lulu expressed no remorse for having killed Kennedy. Asked if she had good reasons for the murder, she proclaimed angrily, "I guess I did have good reasons."

Lulu seemed more concerned about guarding her reputation for morality than she was about the murder charge against her. She denounced as falsehoods the gossip that was swirling around her. Some of the rumors centered on a trip she'd allegedly taken to Chicago and New York in late 1900 and multiple trips she'd made to St. Louis. The insinuation was that she'd made the trips for the purpose of obtaining or trying to obtain an abortion. Lulu denied that she'd made the out-of-state trip and claimed that she'd never been to St. Louis in her life. "Until this trouble happened," she added, "not one word could be said against me."[143]

On the same day that the *Times* reporter visited Lulu at the jail, a *Kansas City Journal* reporter called on her brother Will at the same location. Will placed at least part of the blame for the murder on Kennedy himself because he'd betrayed Lulu and refused to live with her. "She brooded over it," young Prince explained, "until she was wrought up to the pitch in which she killed him. Lulu is a peculiar girl…who gives her whole soul to whatever she adopts." According to Will, Lulu was never very interested in boys and wasn't even particularly struck on Phillip Kennedy when he first started courting her. She soon fell head over heels in love with him, though, and he was very devoted to her as well—until he betrayed her. For the longest time, Will said, Lulu kept Kennedy's seduction and jilting of her secret because she was concerned about what Will and their father might do to the young man, but they finally pried it out of her when she kept acting despondent.[144]

Lulu's trial got underway in early June, and the prosecutor, Herbert S. Hadley (later governor of Missouri), outlined the state's case in his opening statement. The prosecution would prove that, although Kennedy and Lulu Prince met each other about two years earlier and kept company during 1899 and early 1900, Kennedy had broken off the relationship in April 1900 when Will Prince went to him and demanded to know whether he had serious intentions of marrying his sister. Lulu and Kennedy saw each other after that only a couple of times prior to the wedding in early December, but Lulu scarcely brooded over their breakup. Throughout the summer of 1900, she had carried on what the prosecution called a torrid affair with Case Patten, the professional baseball player. In the fall, Patten left Kansas City to return to his home in New York. Shortly afterward, Lulu went to the police seeking to retrieve a ring that she had given Patten, but when she was unable to get it back through official channels, she went to New York herself in mid-October and got the ring. Shortly after she got back, Lulu went to Dr. Cross and told him she was the wife of Case Patten.[145]

According to the state, Kennedy had never "wronged" or seduced Lulu Kennedy. In fact, Lulu herself had told newspaper reporters and others that such was the case. Instead, the motivation for the forced marriage and ultimately for the murder was simply that Lulu was angry and wanted revenge for Kennedy's leaving her for another woman. Also, she wanted to hide her shameful affair with Patten behind the cloak of respectability that a marriage to Kennedy would give her. The state sought to prove, too, that Lulu had not acted entirely on her own but rather in conspiracy with her father and two brothers.[146]

C.H. Nearing, Lulu's lead lawyer, begged to differ. Citing a history of mental illness in Lulu's family, Nearing outlined a defense of emotional insanity brought on by the wrongs that Kennedy had visited upon her. Kennedy had met Lulu over two years earlier and started courting her. As their affection for each other grew, he spent more and more time with Lulu. Eventually, he proposed marriage, and she accepted. When they discussed a date for the wedding, Kennedy asked that it be postponed for a time, but he continued his attentions to Lulu and finally "succeeded in inducing her to yield to him." After seducing Lulu, Kennedy grew cold toward her, and Lulu became distraught, even more so when she discovered that she was "in a delicate condition." Nearing said the ring that Lulu gave Case Patten was for another girl that Patten was seeing and that Kennedy knew about the ring. Lulu had never been intimate with Patten, and retrieving the ring she had given him was just a pretext for her trip back east in October. The trip had actually been at Kennedy's instigation so that she "could be treated for the condition for which Kennedy was responsible." When she came back home, she was still in the same condition as when she left, and that's when she went to see Dr. Cross, again at Kennedy's suggestion. She used an alias (Mrs. Patten), yet again at Kennedy's suggestion, to protect both their reputations. After the marriage, Kennedy grew colder still toward Lulu. He began to cast aspersions on her character and even suggested at one point that she go to live in a disreputable house. Lulu's father and brothers, Nearing declared, knew nothing of the seduction until just before the wedding and did not know about the pregnancy until just before the murder.[147]

On rebuttal, Hadley said that Kennedy was not responsible for Lulu's ruin and that the defense's claim bearing on her reputation for chastity would force the prosecution to introduce evidence about that subject as well. Lulu had intimate relations with not only Patten, but also other men, both before and after she dated Kennedy, almost up to the time of the forced marriage. Kennedy had not seduced Lulu, and moreover, she was not pregnant but had merely been treated for a stomach condition.[148]

The testimony phase of the trial took over a week, and the Kansas City newspapers covered the proceedings in minute detail. Immense crowds packed the courtroom almost every day to witness what many considered the most sensational criminal case in the city's history. After several ballots, the jury came back on June 15 with a verdict finding Lulu guilty of murder in the second degree.[149]

Immediately after the verdict, Nearing said he intended to ask for a new trial and, failing that, appeal to the supreme court. He said he was disappointed that considerable evidence he hoped to introduce had been disallowed by the judge. For instance, at least a couple of different acquaintances of Phillip Kennedy were prepared to testify that Kennedy had admitted to them that he had seduced Lulu. However, the judge ruled that such hearsay testimony would not be allowed unless Lulu was willing to take the stand and swear to that fact herself, and the defense thought she was in no condition to testify on her own behalf.[150]

Rumors began circulating just a day or so after the verdict that Lulu Prince Kennedy might go into theater once she was released, but she said she had no aspirations to go on stage, as she'd had all the notoriety she wanted.[151]

The trial judge denied Lulu a new trial, but she was released on bond on July 30, pending the defense's appeal to the supreme court. Meanwhile, her father and her brother Bert, who had been indicted as accessories to her crime, were also released on bond, while Will remained in jail in lieu of bond.[152]

Will Prince's trial in February 1902 for being complicit in Kennedy's murder resulted in a guilty verdict on a reduced charge of fourth-degree manslaughter, and he was sentenced to two years in prison.[153]

In early July 1903, the Missouri Supreme Court overturned Lulu's conviction and remanded the case to Jackson County for retrial. Two reasons cited for the reversal were that the trial court improperly allowed the prosecution to attack Lulu's character without introducing evidence to support the accusations and that the trial court should not have allowed the prosecution to introduce evidence of a conspiracy between Lulu and her family members when no charge of conspiracy was made in the indictment. A month and a half later, Lulu's brother Will was pardoned by the governor and released from the state penitentiary after serving about eighteen months of his two-year sentence.[154]

The charges against Lulu's father and her brother Bert were dropped not long after she was granted a new trial. Bert drowned at Port Townsend, Washington, in early January 1904 while on a concert tour.[155]

At Lulu's second trial in late January 1904, the state's case was similar to what it had presented at her first trial. Prosecutors argued that not only was Lulu not pregnant as she claimed or intimated at the time she killed her husband but also that Kennedy had never seduced or wronged her. To back up this claim, they called to the stand two different newspaper reporters to whom Lulu admitted that she had not had intimate relations with Kennedy but simply wanted revenge for his having dumped her and that she wanted to "beat the time" of the other young woman to whom Kennedy had recently become engaged.[156]

The defense, however, presented a stronger case for insanity than it had at Lulu's first trial. Her lawyers placed into evidence documents showing that her grandfather, great-grandfather, five uncles, and one aunt, all on her father's side, had died insane in state asylums. Witness after witness testified that Lulu was bright and cheerful as a young girl; that Kennedy had courted her in earnest for almost two years; that she fell deeply in love with him; and that she became nervous, morose, and peculiar in her behavior in the fall of 1900 after he abandoned her. One of the defense witnesses was Lulu's mother, and she caused quite a stir when she revealed from the witness stand that Lulu's name was now Mrs. Kramer. In February 1903, while free on bond, Lulu had married attorney John Kramer, who was part of the defense team in Will Prince's case, and Kramer had been living at the Prince home ever since.[157]

On rebuttal, the state called several doctors who testified that they considered Lulu sane and several other witnesses who testified that they met Lulu in the fall of 1900 and thought she seemed normal. Because of the supreme court's ruling in overturning the first verdict, the judge would not allow prosecutors to introduce evidence of Lulu's alleged romance with Case Patten while she was supposedly pining over Kennedy.[158]

On January 29, 1904, the jurors came back with the following verdict: "We, the jury, find the defendant not guilty on the sole ground that she was insane at the time she shot the deceased; and the jury further finds that she has since recovered her sanity." During an informal discussion, the jurors were initially split ten for acquittal and two for some sort of light sentence, but on the first formal ballot, the vote for acquittal was unanimous.[159]

Although Lulu had once said she had no aspirations to go on stage, just a little over a month after her acquittal, a report circulated that she had been cast as the lead in a melodrama called *The Injured Wife*. The injured husband, however, would not appear in the cast, said the dubious report.[160]

So, did Phillip Kennedy truly "wrong" Lulu Prince by seducing her, getting her pregnant, and then jilting her, as the defense claimed at her trial? Or did she kill her husband simply to get revenge for his having left her for another young woman, as the state claimed?

In denying that Kennedy had seduced Lulu, the state made much of the fact that Lulu herself had told more than one reporter that the two of them had never been intimate. However, what prosecutors failed to mention was that Lulu might have lied to the reporters. The whole reason she sought the interviews with the reporters was because she was concerned that previous newspaper reports had cast doubt on her moral character and she wanted to set the record straight. As one newspaper observed shortly after Lulu was arrested for killing her husband, she seemed more concerned about her reputation for chastity than about the fact that she was accused of murder. So, it is not unreasonable to think that, before the killing, she might have denied having ever been intimate with Kennedy when, in fact, she had been.

Whether she was ever pregnant is a whole different matter. She was definitely not "in a delicate condition" when she was arrested, as she had given her family and others to understand, because from the time she was locked up until she was released on bond, she did not give birth, have a miscarriage, or show any evidence of being with child. Perhaps she had previously been pregnant but had managed to obtain an abortion; she did admit during her last visit to Dr. Cross that she had been to see another doctor since her previous visit to Cross. No matter whether Lulu killed her husband out of unfounded anger or was driven to commit the deed by his mistreatment of her, one thing seems relatively certain. Her actions were at least somewhat insane—enough so that the second jury acquitted her on the basis of that plea.

7
ALWAYS THE SMILE
THE REMORSELESS AGGIE MYERS

In the wee hours of Wednesday morning, May 11, 1904, two Black men broke into the home of twenty-year-old Clarence Myers at 2313 Terrace Street in Kansas City and attacked Myers and his twenty-one-year-old wife, Aggie, in their bed. One of the intruders choked and knocked Aggie senseless as she cowered in a corner of the room. Meanwhile, her husband struggled with the other attacker into an adjoining dining room, where the villain slashed Clarence's throat in three places and left him dead or dying on the floor. The police were not alerted until daylight, when a neighbor heard Aggie's cries and found her lying at the back door, where she'd crawled from the bedroom.[161]

At least that was the story Aggie told, but authorities had their doubts almost from the beginning. When they showed up, they found the Myers home in total disorder, one of the worst crime scenes they'd ever been called to witness. The bed had been broken down and a mattress tossed aside. A kerosene lamp and other items had been knocked to the floor. Blood was splattered on the walls, tables, and chairs of the dining room, and half of a small carpet was pooled with blood. Furniture and clothes had been rifled through, but if robbery were the motive, the intruders had gotten but little. Some change was taken from the dead man's pockets, and twenty-five dollars were taken from Aggie's pocketbook. However, Clarence's gold watch in the pocket of a vest that hung from a chair was not taken.[162]

There were a number of other troubling inconsistencies. A jewelry box that Aggie said was stolen from her bureau was later found secreted in an organ. And why had the McGowan family, who lived next door with no more than four or five feet separating the two houses, not been aroused by the life-and-death struggle that had seemingly occurred? The open bedroom windows of the two houses faced each other and were so close that a person could reach from one to the other. Myers's body was leaning against a wall, but the blood evidence suggested he'd been killed elsewhere in the room. In fact, police thought the whole scene looked as if it had been staged. Also, the killers had taken time after the crime to try to clean up some of the blood and even laid newspapers over some of the blood stains. Why would they do that, investigators wondered. To top it off, when a doctor examined the victim's body, he said he thought, based on the advanced state of rigor mortis, that the man had been dead since midnight or earlier, at least two or three hours before Aggie had said the crime was committed.[163]

Aggie's robe was covered with blood when she was found in the doorway, but she appeared otherwise unhurt. So, she was taken to the police station for questioning. Authorities learned that Alice "Aggie" Brock had come to Kansas City from Ray County about four years earlier with her parents. She was briefly married to a man named Payne, but the couple divorced a few months before Aggie married Myers. Throughout her interrogation, Aggie clung to her story that two Black men had broken in and killed Clarence. She said she did not get a good look at the assailants because they had put out the lamp when they first entered and she was soon knocked unconscious. About all she recalled for certain was that they were Black and one was considerably larger than the other one. She explained the misplaced jewelry box by saying that she often hid it in different places and simply forgot where she'd put it.[164]

Although the detectives who questioned Aggie thought she knew more than she was letting on about her husband's murder, she was released the next day, and the police's official position was that they were still operating under the theory that burglars had committed the crime. Before leaving the police station, Aggie gave a statement that was published the next day in a Kansas City newspaper:

> *I cannot imagine why anyone would suspect that I had any hand in my husband's death. He was the best of husbands. He gave me all the money he earned; he was attentive to me; he loved his home; he worked hard.... Tuesday evening, we sat on the front porch talking and laughing, in the very best of humor. There wasn't the faintest suspicion of a quarrel. There could be no earthly reason why I should wish for his death.*[165]

Sketch of Aggie Myers. *From the Kansas City Journal.*

After her release, Aggie went to stay with her parents at another location in Kansas City. One of the first things she did on arriving there was to send word to her neighbors, the McGowans, for them to tell the postman to leave any letters for Aggie or her dead husband with them rather than deliver the letters to the Myers house. When the police learned of this request, they thought it odd. What sort of letter might Aggie be expecting that she didn't want left at her old home? Also, it seemed unusual that, although Aggie visited her dead husband at the undertaker's rooms and shed a few tears, she declined an invitation from Clarence's father to accompany the Myers family back to Newton, Kansas, for the funeral the following day. Aggie said she was too "broken down" by the affair to make the trip.[166]

To a newspaper reporter, Aggie repeated her story of the crime, almost exactly as she'd told it to police. Asked whether she was sure the intruders "were negroes," she said, yes, she was sure, and they were very black.[167]

On May 20, two Black men were arrested on suspicion of knowing something about the Myers murder, but when Aggie Myers was brought to the police station to view them, she said they were not the men who had killed her husband.[168]

After the Myers inquest, which had previously been postponed, was once again continued at the request of police on May 27, nothing more was heard about the Myers case for over a month, but then in early July, word reached Kansas City that twenty-year-old Frank Hottman had been arrested in Walla Walla, Washington, and charged with the murder of Clarence Myers. Police said that Hottman, a childhood friend of Aggie Myers, had been a person of interest in the case early on. He had visited the Myers home and had been seen with Aggie elsewhere in Kansas City in the days leading up to the crime, and on the Sunday prior to the murder, the two had been buggy riding together at Higginsville, their childhood home. Then, the day after the crime, Hottman had left town. His movements before and after the crime cast immediate suspicion on him, and shortly after the murder, some bloody cuffs and other fragments of men's clothing found in a cistern at the Myers home were linked to Hottman. Authorities had been hot on his trail ever since.[169]

Interviewed in Washington while awaiting extradition, Hottman denied involvement in the murder. He admitted that Aggie Myers had met him at the train station when he came from Higginsville a few days before the murder, that they'd seen each other clandestinely several times in the days leading up to the crime, and even that Aggie had sat on his lap one time when he visited her at her house while her husband was at work. However, he said he'd known Aggie for ten years and that they'd never been more than friends. Like his story of his friendship with Aggie, his story of his departure from Kansas City also seemed contradictory. He claimed to have left town before the murder, but he couldn't seem to say whether he'd left in daytime or darkness and gave conflicting statements about the route he'd taken in coming to Walla Walla. He admitted the circumstances looked bad for him, but he claimed to know nothing of the murder.[170]

After Hottman was arrested in Walla Walla, Aggie Myers was again taken into custody in Kansas City. A day or two later, she gave a statement reiterating that her husband's murder was committed by two Black men. Echoing what Hottman had said, she claimed that the two of them were just good friends, as any two people who'd known each other most of their lives might be. She admitted going buggy riding with Hottman in Higginsville on the Sunday before the murder, but she said nobody in Higginsville thought anything about it at the time, because everybody knew the two of them were just friends. However, her statement seemed to contradict what Hottman had said in at least one respect. She claimed he had not been to her house in Kansas City for over two weeks prior to the murder, whereas Hottman had suggested otherwise.[171]

Aggie's denials mattered little, because near the same time that she gave her statement, Frank Hottman, back in Washington, "weakened" and confessed to the murder. He said that he and Aggie were in love and that she had planned the crime so that they could get married. He said he hated to commit the crime because Clarence Myers had always been friendly to him but that Aggie urged him to do it. He came to Kansas City from Higginsville intending to kill Clarence. After a couple of days, during which he visited in the Myers home, he again came to Aggie's house in the wee hours of May 11. She was waiting up for him, and they went together to Clarence's room planning to kill him in his sleep. However, he awoke when they entered the room, sprang up, and demanded to know what Hottman was doing there again. Hottman hit Myers over the head with a club made from the heavy end of a billiard cue and then held him in a clinch while Aggie slashed his throat with a razor.[172]

Sketch depicting Aggie's murder of her husband. *From the Kansas City Journal.*

Told of Hottman's confession, Aggie maintained her innocence. She said she thought the confession must have been coerced. Even after she was confronted with all the evidence the police had gathered contradicting what she'd told them, she stubbornly clung to her story.[173]

Despite her protestations of innocence, Aggie, who previously had been held merely for questioning, was officially arrested on a charge of first-degree murder. The officers who interviewed Aggie or otherwise interacted with her were struck by her stoic manner. No matter how hard she was grilled, Aggie remained calm, looked her interrogators in the eye, and, with the hint of a smile, coolly denied their accusations. "Always the smile," said a newspaper reporter who interviewed her. One officer, while holding a silver-handled umbrella, remarked, "She's as cold and immovable as this handle." Aggie clung to her story of two intruders, although she now allowed that Hottman, made up to look Black, might have been one of the assailants. Why in the world he would want to implicate Aggie, though, she couldn't venture to say.[174]

Brought back from Washington, Hottman arrived in Kansas City on July 12. Elaborating on the confession he'd given in Washington, the prisoner said that, on the night of the murder, Myers appealed to his wife for help. The last words he said were "Honey, help me!" Asked whether Mrs. Myers did, in fact, help her husband, Hottman replied, "Yes, she helped him. She cut his throat from ear to ear with the first slash of the razor."[175]

A couple of days later, however, Hottman's attorney denied that his client had ever confessed to killing Clarence Myers. The lawyer said the police had put out the false confessions in an effort to trap Aggie Myers. In rebuttal, the *Kansas City Star* let its readers know that there was no doubt that Hottman had confessed, not once but three different times. A *Star* reporter had seen and read the written confession Hottman gave after he was brought back to Kansas City.[176]

On the morning of August 1, a crowd estimated at three thousand, most of them women, gathered outside the criminal court in Kansas City in anticipation of Aggie and Hottman's arraignment, and when the doors opened, they made a mad rush to get inside, shoving and jostling each other to get the best seats. The officers in charge had to separate several people who were fighting over seats. Many people, unable to get seats in the courtroom, filled the stairways and halls of the building, and hundreds more were turned away. When the "trim figure" of Aggie Myers, "neatly dressed all in black," was ushered into the room, many in the courtroom surged forward to get a better look at her. "They ogled her and fairly devoured her with their eyes." Through it all, Aggie remained "absolutely unruffled and cool." When the judge asked her how she pleaded, she answered, "I am not guilty."[177]

The spectators were curious to see Hottman, too, but there was "a long sigh of disappointment when he was brought in." Whereas "Mrs. Myers was tolerably good looking and no one could say she did not carry herself with dignity," Hottman "was a low-browed fellow with a large, hulking, awkward frame and extremely ill featured." He met "the crowd's ideal of what a murderer ought to look like." Both his and Aggie's trials were set for November.[178]

However, the two cases were severed, and after several postponements, Hottman's trial began in January 1905. In addition to offering the defendant's multiple confessions into evidence, the state paraded several witnesses to the stand to establish the intimate relationship between Hottman and Aggie Myers prior to the murder. One witness, for example, testified that Hottman and Mrs. Myers had rented a room at a rooming house together a few days before the murder. Prosecutors also presented several key items of evidence. These included the bloody cuffs and a bloody hat belonging to Hottman that were found at the Myers place after the crime and a hat Hottman was wearing at the time he was arrested in Walla Walla that had belonged to Clarence Myers.[179]

The only defense presented by Hottman's lawyers consisted mainly of a plea for mercy and an attack on the police for their supposedly heavy-handed tactics in coercing a confession from the defendant. Aside from empaneling a jury, the trial consumed only one day, and the jury came back on the evening of January 13 after only four minutes of deliberation with a verdict of first-degree murder and a sentence of death.[180]

Aggie Myers was granted a change of venue to Clay County for her trial, and it was held at Liberty in early June. Much of the testimony and evidence presented was similar to that given during Hottman's trial. Whenever testimony against her was being given, Aggie remained just as stoic and impassive as ever. She "kept her brown eyes beaded on every witness," sometimes glancing at the jurors long enough to see how they were reacting to some damning bit of testimony. Just as often the jurors looked at her to see what effect the damaging statements were having on her, but according to the *Kansas City Journal*, "they might as well have expected the walls to change color or expression," because, even as the goriest details of her alleged crime were being recited, Aggie showed "not the least tinge of emotion or excitement."[181]

The climax of the trial came when Frank Hottman took the stand as a state witness, spoke of the conspiracy between him and Aggie to kill her husband, and recounted the horrific details of the crime. Prior to this moment, many people had seemed to side with Aggie, but Hottman's damning statement turned the tide against her. After the state rested, Aggie took the stand in her own defense, but her tired story of two Black intruders recaptured little of the sympathy she'd lost.[182]

The jury was given the case on the evening of June 10, and they came back the next day with a verdict finding Aggie guilty of murder

STATEMENT BY AGGIE MYERS.

To the Public:

I maintain my innocence of the murder of my husband, and have hopes of getting acquitted. I believe the jury will understand from the evidence given here that I am not guilty and that a scheme has been fixed up to save Frank Hottman's neck. I never talked to Frank Hottman about killing Clarence and all his testimony was false. I expect to get free, and am glad I went to trial.

Aggie Myers.

County Jail, Liberty, Mo., 6 p. m., June 9, 1905.

One of several public statements Aggie Myers made declaring her innocence, this one from the Clay County Jail, while awaiting trial. *From the Kansas City Journal.*

in the first degree. On the first ballot, the vote stood nine to three for conviction, but the final holdout for acquittal was won over on the fourth ballot. When the verdict was announced, Aggie accepted the news with the same aplomb she'd exhibited throughout the entire proceedings against her. One commentator remarked that Aggie's self-possession was so marvelous that it was a wonder why her attorneys had not put it forth as proof of her insanity.[183]

In late June, Aggie's motion for a new trial was denied, and the judge sentenced her to hang on August 11. The sentence was suspended, however, pending her appeal to the Missouri Supreme Court. In late May 1906, the high court affirmed the death sentences of both Hottman and Mrs. Myers and set the date of execution for June 29.[184]

Missouri Governor Joseph Folk was inundated with letters from throughout the state about Aggie's case. The majority pleaded for mercy on her behalf, but a good number insisted that the sentence be carried out. In mid-June, the high court denied a defense motion that Aggie's case be reconsidered, but the governor granted a reprieve of her and Hottman's sentences while he considered their case.[185]

Folk later granted another respite, and during the delay, Aggie and her case continued to draw a lot of attention throughout Missouri and the entire country. Numerous men even expressed a willingness to marry her if and when she ever got released, but according to the *Kansas City Times*, the women were "unaccountably slow in offering themselves to Frank Hottman."[186]

Aggie's lawyers continued working tirelessly on her behalf, but the state supreme court denied both a motion to have the full court hear her case and a motion for a writ of error that would allow the attorneys to take the case to the U.S. Supreme Court. Her lawyers then appealed directly to U.S. Supreme Court Justice David Brewer, who ordered a temporary reprieve to give the lawyers a chance to present their case more fully, and the execution date was postponed yet again.[187]

Brewer denied the appeal on December 8, two days before the scheduled execution, but Governor Folk promptly granted yet another stay. In response to the latest reprieve, some observers said the repeated stays of execution constituted cruel and unusual punishment and urged Governor Folk that, if he was going to commute Aggie's and Hottman's sentences, he ought to go ahead and do so immediately.[188]

A writ of habeas corpus filed by Aggie's attorneys was denied in federal court in Kansas City in early January 1907, but their application for an appeal of the decision to the entire U.S. Supreme Court was granted.

The last-minute reprieve barely prevented Aggie's execution, because the sheriff of Clay County was already at work on the scaffold and did not receive notice of the stay until the evening before Aggie was supposed to be dropped into eternity.[189]

Sketch of Aggie Myers as she was leaving for the state penitentiary. *From the Kansas City Star.*

On April 8, before Aggie's case could be heard in the U.S. Supreme Court, Governor Folk finally commuted both her and Hottman's sentences from execution to life imprisonment. (Aggie's attorneys subsequently dismissed their appeal to the highest court in the land.) When Aggie got the news of the commutation of her sentence, she expressed appreciation to Governor Folk and said she still hoped to prove her innocence.[190]

Aggie Myers was transported from Liberty to the state penitentiary at Jefferson City on April 19, 1907. She passed through Kansas City dressed in a stylish new outfit and carrying a bouquet of flowers.[191]

Frank Hottman died in prison in September 1923. Aggie, meanwhile, spent another sixteen months in prison before being paroled in January 1925 after serving over twenty years behind bars, including her time in county jails. After her release, she returned to Kansas City. She later married a druggist and moved to Colorado.[192]

8
ALMOST LIKE A TIGRESS
THE STORY OF ANNIE HUNNING

About eight o'clock on Saturday evening, December 9, 1911, thirty-six-year-old Martin Hunning, a farmer living in an isolated area on Sugar Creek Road (now Old Sugar Creek Road) south of Murphy in Jefferson County, Missouri, arose from the kitchen table and went to the telephone to call a neighbor. The phone, which had been installed just the day before, was situated near a window, and as Hunning was waiting for the central switchboard to connect him to his neighbor, somebody fired a shotgun through the window. The blast tore half of Hunning's head off, and he fell instantly dead. Hunning's thirty-five-year-old wife, Anna (a.k.a. Annie), rushed to the door of the two-room cabin and heard a man's voice she did not recognize say, "We've got to beat it. They've got a telephone."[193]

From that statement, Annie deduced that there must have been two men involved in the murder, but it was too dark for her to see. Turning back in fright, she stepped over her husband's dead body to the telephone and called for help. Then she "dropped in a swoon."[194]

At least that was what she told neighbors who answered her summons and found her "lying in a faint." She added, "I have no idea what the cause of the attack was. Martin was born and raised here and, so far as I know, had no enemies. He was popular because of his good nature. There was no attempt at robbery."[195]

According to a local doctor, who was one of the people summoned, none of the neighbors who arrived on the scene expressed "any suspicion as to the cause of the assassination," and the doctor later told a St. Louis newspaper that the murder was "a complete mystery."[196]

Volunteers patrolled the roads around the Hunning home throughout the night, and a search party was organized at first light on Sunday morning. From tracks around the window, investigators deduced that there had been only one person involved in the murder, not two as Mrs. Hunning had suggested. Bloodhounds were brought to the scene and put on the trail of the killer, but the dogs lost the scent as they were circling around and came to the edge of a cliff. Investigators theorized that the murderer had ridden to the cliff on horseback, dismounted to commit the murder, and then returned to the horse afterward, which accounted for the dogs' sudden loss of the killer's scent.[197]

By Monday evening, the posse that was organized to search for Hunning's killer had disbanded, although volunteers continued to search as individuals. On Tuesday, December 12, Hunning's funeral was held at the High Ridge Lutheran Church, where the dead man's widow and his elderly mother were "the chief mourners."[198]

One of the theories floated in the aftermath of the murder was that the assassin was an ex-convict whom Hunning, as a member of a posse, had shot and wounded many years earlier, leading to the man's arrest and imprisonment. The man was said to have sworn revenge at the time, but he had been out of prison for several years. Why would he wait so long?[199]

Meanwhile, Jefferson County prosecuting attorney Albert Miller, who placed little stock in the ex-convict notion, was developing his own theory. "I believe there is a whole lot more to this affair than has yet been brought out," he said. He announced that he planned to personally visit the scene of the crime and that there might be "some surprising developments."[200]

A coroner's jury returned an open verdict, concluding only that Hunning had been killed by an unknown party or parties. Despite the inconclusive inquest, both the county coroner and the county sheriff shared Miller's opinion that the ex-convict theory was weak.[201]

The "surprising development" in the case that the prosecutor had promised came on Thursday, December 14, four and a half days after the murder, when twenty-eight-year-old Joseph Seidl, a neighbor of the Hunnings, was arrested as a result of "neighborhood gossip" that had been spreading since Sunday morning connecting him to the Hunnings in an "eternal triangle."[202]

Seidl was taken for questioning to Hillsboro, the Jefferson County seat, where he denied any knowledge of or involvement in Hunning's murder, and he was released after several hours of interrogation. Informed of Seidl's arrest, Mrs. Hunning exclaimed, "He did not do it. I know he did not do it." She had previously told investigators that Seidl and another young man had been at the Hunning place cutting wood on the Saturday afternoon prior to the murder and that Seidl had left about five thirty after eating supper with her and her husband, but she declined to say why she was certain that Seidl had nothing to do with Martin's murder.[203]

Asked about the state of her and her husband's marital relations, Annie denied that there had been any "domestic infelicity" in the household. She admitted, however, that Seidl was a frequent visitor in the Hunning home.[204]

Although Seidl's release marked a setback in the investigation, Prosecutor Miller remained dogged in his determination to ferret out the facts behind the murder. On December 18, just over a week after the crime, he announced that, based on new leads he'd come up with, he had ordered the exhumation of Hunning's body for the purpose of convening a new coroner's inquest into the man's death. Miller said he planned to question everybody in the Hunning neighborhood in order to "run down a lot of gossip" and "find out exactly what every person thereabouts knows" in relation to the murder. The prosecutor said he had a pretty good idea who had committed the murder, but he would not reveal the suspect's name, pending the outcome of the new inquest.[205]

The next day, December 19, the body was exhumed at the cemetery and viewed by the coroner's jury to satisfy a formality of law. The dead man was immediately reinterred, and the new inquest began at a nearby fraternal lodge, converted into a makeshift courtroom. Annie Hunning was among those who testified before the jury, which was made up of men who were not from the Hunning neighborhood and had not been on the previous jury. Annie repeated the story she'd told from the beginning: her husband was shot down by someone unknown to her as he stood at the window talking on the telephone. Questioned about her friendship with Seidl, she admitted that he had visited her home not only on the day of the murder when her husband was present but also the day before the crime, when Hunning was not there. Still, she denied that a romantic relationship existed between her and Seidl.[206]

Several neighbors of the Hunnings, however, testified that Annie Hunning's reputation for morality was not good and that Martin Hunning had expressed concern over her behavior, in particular her seemingly close friendship with Seidl. The first day of the inquest ended with several more witnesses still to be called.[207]

Left: Annie Hunning, who conspired with Joe Seidl to kill her husband. *From the St. Louis Post-Dispatch.*

Right: Joe Seidl. *From the St. Louis Star and Times.*

The next day, December 20, Annie Hunning was placed back on the stand, and when Prosecutor Miller asked her point-blank whether she and Seidl had conspired to kill her husband, she denied the accusation. Seidl, who had not appeared at the inquest the previous day, was then called, and he, too, denied Miller's accusation that he had killed Martin Hunning in conspiracy with the victim's wife. Several other witnesses, though, gave damning testimony, including Annie's own father, who said he'd witnessed an angry confrontation between his son-in-law and Seidl the previous summer. At the end of the inquest, Annie Hunning and Joseph Seidl were arrested at the recommendation of the coroner's jury. The prisoners were taken by wagon to Hillsboro and lodged in the Jefferson County Jail. Following his arrest, Seidl declared that he'd never paid anything but honorable attention to Annie Hunning, stressing that he'd never even sat close to her when he visited in her home, and he said he expected to be exonerated.[208]

On Saturday evening, December 23, John Keeley, a St. Louis detective who was known for his ability to "sweat" suspects into confessing, came to Hillsboro at Prosecutor Miller's request to question Joseph Seidl. The prisoner was under the "third degree" for nineteen hours, from Saturday evening until early Sunday afternoon, before he finally broke down and admitted that he and Annie Hunning had, indeed, had amorous relations. "Yes, she loved me," he whispered. "She loved me. She told me that if her husband could be got rid of, she and I could be happy." Seidl said he'd been seeing Annie secretly about two or three times a week, whenever her husband was away from home, for almost a year. Although Seidl said Annie loved him, he said he did not to love her and didn't want to marry her, but he was "fascinated by her." Seeking to put the blame for their illicit affair squarely on Annie, Seidl later said, "She tempted me, and I yielded." Despite his admission of a romantic relationship with Annie, Seidl still claimed that he did not kill Martin Hunning. Keeley thought he might be telling the truth on that score, because he didn't think Seidl had the nerve or gumption for it.[209]

Keeley also interrogated Annie Hunning, but she refused to break. She not only denied that she had conspired to kill her husband, but she also insisted that she and Seidl had never been romantically involved. Confronted with Seidl's confession, she did not wince and immediately condemned Seidl as a "contemptible liar and a coward." Keeley said afterward, "Of all the women I have known, I think that Mrs. Hunning has the strongest will. It is marvelous the way she glared at me and persisted in professing her innocence. Almost like a tigress, she eyed me defiantly."[210]

Seidl's confession of intimate relations with Annie Hunning was written down, sworn to by the prisoner, and later released for publication.[211]

When R.A. Frazier, one of Seidl and Mrs. Hunning's lawyers, learned of Seidl's confession, he protested that the confession should be thrown out because it was given under extreme duress without counsel present. Also, he argued that the confession amounted to little anyway, because Seidl had merely admitted to a romantic relationship with Mrs. Hunning, not to murdering her husband.[212]

Although Prosecutor Miller claimed that Seidl and Mrs. Hunning had not been mistreated, he conceded, after their lawyer's protest, that Mrs. Hunning would not be subjected to further "sweating." He didn't think it would be productive anyway, because, like Keeley, he was convinced she would not break. "She is a remarkable woman—a very remarkable woman," he said. "Her will is indomitable."[213]

Miller did not introduce Seidl's confession into evidence at Seidl and Mrs. Hunning's preliminary hearing before Justice W.L. Stone at Hillsboro on December 29 but relied, instead, on the testimony of other witnesses to establish the intimate relationship between the defendants. Miller outlined how Annie had planned the murder of her husband with Seidl when he visited her on the night before the crime; the next night, she had placed her sewing machine in a strategic location with a lamp sitting on it so that Seidl could see through the window when Hunning came to the telephone. She had then blown the lamp out as a signal for Seidl to fire. Attorney Frazier countered that Miller was merely advancing a theory that was not supported by the evidence. Just because Seidl might have danced with Annie Hunning at a picnic, for instance, did not mean that they had an intimate relationship and certainly not that they had conspired to kill Martin Hunning.[214]

Despite what Frazier saw as a thin thread of evidence, Justice Stone, after the hearing, ordered that the defendants be held without bond to await the action of a grand jury. The next day, however, Prosecutor Miller announced that he had sufficient evidence to file an information charging Joseph Seidl and Annie Hunning with first-degree murder without waiting for the grand jury. He said he planned to take the case straight to trial, where he would introduce Seidl's confession, which he had withheld from evidence at the preliminary.[215]

Miller filed the information in early January 1912, and the trial was set for March. Although he had earlier declared that he thought further interrogation of Annie Hunning would be fruitless, Miller changed his mind when a trusty, who had acted as a go-between for Seidl and Mrs. Hunning since their incarceration, turned over some love notes that the two prisoners had exchanged. One such note, from Annie to Seidl dated January 14, read as follows:

> *Honey, I did not think you had nerve to do it. Do you think we get free? It is your fault as much as mine. I think you said more than what you ought to* [have] *said. Did you? I hope you won't go against me honey. I won't go against you in here. I would not care what money it take if we go free. That way I think of it. I think we get stuck on it because you told too much, did you? Honey goodbye. 15 kisses.*[216]

Armed with the incriminating notes, Miller grilled Annie for six straight hours, and finally, shortly after midnight on January 15, she broke down and admitted that she had foreknowledge of her husband's murder. She said she had told Seidl that her husband might kill both of them and that Seidl had taken it upon himself to take care of Martin.

Annie downplayed her own complicity in the murder and tried to lay most of the blame on Seidl.[217]

Confronted with the love notes and told of Annie's confession, Seidl begged to differ. He gave and signed a statement saying that she was in on the crime from the beginning and had set the stage by placing her sewing machine near the window with a lighted lamp on it, which he used to guide his aim for the murderous shotgun blast, just as Prosecutor Miller had theorized. Miller later explained that the fact that the lamp was not in its normal place in a bracket on the wall when he first visited the murder scene led him to his theory.[218]

A couple of days after signing the confessions, Mrs. Hunning and Seidl repudiated them. Both said they only signed the statements to "end the torment of the 'third degree'" to which they had been subjected and that, even then, they thought they were admitting only that they had been romantically involved, not that they had conspired to kill Annie's husband.[219]

However, Seidl's confession, which was published in full in St. Louis newspapers, was damning in its detail, as were the confiscated love notes.

Seidl's and Mrs. Hunning's cases were severed, and his trial began first, in late March at Hillsboro. The state's evidence was similar to what was presented at the second coroner's jury, except that Seidl's confession was admitted as evidence over strenuous objections from the defense. In addition to opposing admission of the confession on the grounds that it was coerced, the defense argued that the gunshot that killed Hunning could not have come through the south window of the Hunning home as the prosecution's theory of the crime held. In addition, Seidl's lawyer made a case for an insanity plea by introducing testimony that certain members of the Seidl family had suffered from mental problems. The highlight of the defense came when Seidl himself took the stand. He claimed that he was drunk at the time he gave his confession and that he was bullied into giving it. The jury got the case on the late evening of April 2 and came back early the next afternoon with a guilty verdict and a sentence of life imprisonment. The jury reportedly agreed on the guilty verdict from the beginning of deliberations, but it took several ballots before the jurors reached unanimity on the sentence, as three or four initially argued for a death sentence.[220]

Jury selection for Annie Hunning's trial began immediately after Seidl's ended, and testimony began a few days later. The highlight of the prosecution's case was the testimony of surprise witness Joseph Seidl. Annie gasped when Seidl entered the courtroom and took the stand. He said he and

Annie had planned the murder of her husband two months ahead of time. Seidl said that Annie had told him they would get married and she would give him over $1,000 that her husband had in the bank if her husband were out of the way. On cross-examination by the defense, Seidl admitted that Mrs. Hunning never specifically asked him to kill her husband—only that she warned him that her husband might kill him—and that he made the decision on his own to kill Hunning. However, she knew about the plan all along and went along with it.[221]

When the defense presented its case, Annie took the stand to tell her side of the story. Appearing unruffled, she glanced around the room, looked expectantly at her attorney, and recited the same story of the murder that she had told from the beginning about hearing a voice outside her house say, "We got to get out of reach, they have a telephone." Annie admitted that she was "unduly friendly" with Joseph Seidl and that she had told him that her husband might kill both of them, but she claimed not to know that Seidl was the one who had killed Martin.[222]

In his closing argument, Prosecutor Miller compared Annie Hunning to Lady Macbeth and demanded that she be given the death penalty. The jury got the case on April 10 and came back the next morning, after being out almost twenty-four hours, to report that they were hopelessly deadlocked. The vote was reportedly split six for conviction and six for acquittal on the first ballot. Several jurors switched their votes from conviction to acquittal on succeeding ballots, but one holdout for conviction refused to budge, and the final ballot stood eleven to one for acquittal on the final ballot. The judge declared a mistrial and set a new trial date for the defendant.[223]

At Annie's second trial in mid-May, Seidl surprised the prosecution when he took the stand and swore that Annie had nothing at all to do with her husband's murder. Pressed by Miller, however, he finally broke down and repeated much the same story he'd told at her first trial. Annie's testimony in her own defense was also similar to what she'd given at her first trial, denying that she had any foreknowledge of her husband's murder. On May 20, the jury returned a verdict of guilty after only a couple of hours' deliberation and fixed Annie's punishment at life imprisonment. It was later reported that the jury was in unanimous agreement from the beginning that Annie was guilty and that the only deliberations were over whether to sentence her to death or to life in prison.[224]

A week later, Annie and her lover were transferred together to the Missouri State Penitentiary. Annie was paroled in December 1919 after serving only seven and half years of her scheduled life sentence. In January 1921, a group of citizens in the Valley Park area, where Annie now lived, petitioned the governor to have her pardoned and restored to citizenship, and the request was granted the following month. Seidl remained in prison, but he, too, was discharged under parole a year later.[225]

9

CLARA SCHWEIGER OF SPOTTED ADDER SNAKE FAME

Dramatically proclaiming her revenge as she fired, Mrs. Clara T. Schweiger, of spotted adder snake fame, shot and probably fatally wounded her former husband, Louis L. Schweiger, at 11:00 o'clock this morning in the corridor of the first floor of the courthouse. As he fell to the floor, Mrs. Schweiger, struggling in the grip of several bystanders, turned the revolver upon herself and inflicted dangerous wounds.

So read the lead paragraph of a front-page story in the Saturday afternoon, May 1, 1915 edition of the *Kansas City Post.* The reference to the adder snake was an allusion to a strange incident involving Clara Schweiger that had occurred almost six months earlier, but whether the snake episode factored into Clara's ultimate act of "revenge" is not clear.

Louis L. Schweiger and Clara Dulle had married in 1902 when they were twenty-seven and twenty-two years old, respectively. Clara had previously been married to a man named Thomas Cheek, but Cheek deserted her after just six weeks. Schweiger, who had courted Clara prior to her marriage to Cheek, paid for her to get a divorce, and he and Clara were married shortly afterward. To all appearances, the Schweigers seemed happy for the first ten years of their marriage. They had no biological children, but they had an adopted son, Norman, to whom they were both devoted. Trouble in the marriage began about 1912, when gossip spread in the Schweigers' Swope Park neighborhood that Louis was paying attention to another woman. The gossip preyed on Clara's fragile mind, even though there is no solid evidence that there was substantial truth to the rumors, and she grew "very jealous and extremely nervous."[226]

In early 1913, some of the neighbors persuaded Louis to have his wife hospitalized for being "temporarily deranged." Clara later claimed she was suffering only from "nervous prostration," and she blamed her problems on a woman in the neighborhood who had "a kleptomania for other women's husbands."[227]

The friction in the marriage came to a head in early October 1913, when Schweiger, Clara, and their son were taking a streetcar to church. When Schweiger spoke to a neighbor woman on the streetcar, his wife went into a rage, accusing him of being unfaithful. She jumped up and took Norman off the streetcar, and when Schweiger returned home, she and the boy were not there. He tried to get her to come back home, but she wouldn't do it. So, Schweiger, who was vice president of the T.G. Schweiger Construction Company, left his wife and filed for divorce.[228]

The divorce was pending and Clara was back living in the Schweiger home at 3819 East Sixtieth Street with nine-year-old Norman when the postman showed up on November 10, 1914, to deliver the mail. Clara met him at the door, and he handed her a package. "Looks like a box of bon bons," he remarked.[229]

When Clara took the package, she felt something move inside it and said so to the mailman as she handed the parcel back. Together they opened the box, and a small, deadly adder poked its head out. The postman picked up a big rock and smashed the snake to death.[230]

Suffering from "severe nervous shock," Clara admitted to a newspaperman that she'd had trouble in the past with some of the neighbor women. She didn't know whether the past trouble with her neighbors was related to the sending of the snake, but she was convinced that someone was deliberately trying to hurt her.[231]

Schweiger's divorce suit came up in court later that month. The plaintiff said his wife had "an uncontrollable temper," and the suit charged her with "neglect of household duties" and "general indignities." One of the specifications was that his wife would not allow him more than $5 per week spending money because she felt there were too many temptations and pitfalls for men with money. Clara contested the action, saying she did not want a divorce, but it was nonetheless granted and Schweiger was given custody of the couple's son, Norman. Clara was allowed a lump sum alimony of $500.[232]

This sketch of Clara Schweiger was published in the *Kansas City Times* the day after she killed her husband. *From the Kansas City Times.*

In the late winter of 1915, Clara bought an automatic revolver and began carrying it with her. After the purchase, Schweiger's family and friends tried to warn him that his ex-wife might kill him if he wasn't careful, but he just laughed and said that if she wanted to kill him, she'd probably do it whether he was careful or not.[233]

The gossip in the Schweiger neighborhood didn't stop even after the divorce. One rumor, in particular, disturbed Clara. It was known in the neighborhood that when the Schweigers were first contemplating adoption, Louis had wanted a boy, while Clara had favored a girl. Louis's wish had prevailed, the couple had adopted Norman, and Clara had grown to love the boy at least as much as Louis did. But now, years later, a story circulated that Louis had tricked his wife into agreeing to adopt Norman because the boy was, in fact, his biological child and that was why Louis had been granted custody. The whisperings so disturbed Clara that, in late April 1915, she made a trip to Cincinnati to try to learn the truth about Norman's parentage, and she came back satisfied that Louis was not the boy's biological father.[234]

After Louis Schweiger's divorce petition was granted, Clara hired Tiera Farrow, one of Kansas City's first female lawyers, to file a motion on her behalf to annul the divorce. On Saturday morning, May 1, 1915, just a day or two after Clara's return from Cincinnati, the two women showed up at Judge Daniel Bird's courtroom in downtown Kansas City for the hearing. Unknown to Farrow, her client had her automatic revolver secreted inside her purse.[235]

Clara seemed depressed during the proceeding, and Bird's decision to overrule her motion doubtlessly did nothing to alleviate her melancholy. After the case was adjourned, Schweiger and his lawyer went to the first floor and stopped at a cigar counter to purchase cigars. They had turned and started toward an exit when Clara and her attorney, following the men down from the courtroom, emerged from an elevator. When Clara saw her ex-husband, she hastened her step toward him, pulled the revolver from her purse, and called out, "Now I have got you for lying about me."[236]

She came up behind him and shot him three times in the back. Schweiger slumped to the floor, proclaiming that he didn't lie, and begged Clara not to shoot anymore. Ignoring his pleas, she stood over him and pumped at least one more round into his body.[237]

Clara turned around and fired an errant shot toward Schweiger's attorney before several bystanders ran over and seized her. Struggling with them, she momentarily freed herself long enough to fire two shots into her own body.[238]

Tiera Farrow, the lady lawyer who defended Clara Sweiger, in uniform. *Courtesy the Museum of Kansas City Foundation.*

As she sank to the floor, Schweiger struggled to his feet and staggered toward a door before falling again. Meanwhile, Clara sobbed and cried out as she lay writhing on the floor. "I want my boy," she moaned. "I love him."[239]

A police ambulance arrived and whisked the wounded pair away to separate hospitals. Little hope was expressed for Schweiger's recovery, while Clara's wounds were considered serious but not life-threatening.[240]

In a deathbed statement, Schweiger told the assistant prosecuting attorney that Clara had pulled a revolver from her handbag and deliberately shot him. "She threatened to kill me even before I left her," Schweiger continued. "I always thought it was more of a bluff than anything else. I loved her and wanted to do the right thing by her, but she was always so contrary."[241]

Shortly after Clara was brought to the General Hospital, she sent for Father James Keyes, a Catholic priest. Unaware of how gravely wounded her husband was, she asked Keyes to take a message to him: "Tell Louie that I am sorry I did it, and ask him and God to forgive me. I did it because I loved him, but now I am sorry."[242]

Keyes carried the message a block away to the German Hospital, where Schweiger was lingering near death. In answer to the message, Schweiger told the priest, "Tell her that I forgive her and that I always loved her."[243]

Schweiger said he knew he was dying, and he asked to see his son, Norman, one last time. The boy was hurried to the hospital, where Louis told him, "Always be a good boy and take care of your mother now that I am going to die."[244]

Schweiger died at 4:15 p.m., about five hours after he'd been shot. However, Clara was not informed of her husband's death until Monday morning. When she heard the news, she sobbed, moaned hysterically, and begged to die. She told the story, incoherently at times, of how her once happy home had been wrecked by "people who would not let us live and love each other in peace and alone." Consumed by a sense of isolation and loneliness when her last hope of reuniting with her husband and her son was dashed in Judge Bird's courtroom that Saturday morning, she came down the elevator "with a heart that was dead in my breast."[245]

When she saw Louis in the corridor strong and healthy and well-dressed, while she was "a poor, shabby, ill-dressed thing," something snapped inside her. "What chance had I with him? None, none! None at all, and oh God, how I did love him! I worshipped the very ground he walked on. I would have crawled to him on my knees if he had told me to....I wanted him and my baby boy so."[246]

The shooting itself was "all a blur," she said. "I found myself like in a dream with a gun in my hand and my love dying on the floor at my feet."[247]

An information charging Clara with first-degree murder was filed on May 3, and she was removed from the hospital to the county jail on the fourth. Later the same day, when she was taken before a justice for arraignment, she entered a plea of not guilty.[248]

In early June, Clara waived a preliminary hearing, and her trial was set for August but later continued multiple times. When the trial finally got underway in late February 1916, spectators filled the courtroom, drawn not only by the novelty of a woman defendant in a murder case but also by the even more unusual phenomenon of a woman lawyer, Tiera Farrow, as counsel for the defense.[249]

During the state's opening statement, Clara grew hysterical and cried out "This is too much!" when the prosecutor accused her of abusing her deceased husband, calling him names like "devil" and "dirty cur," and repeatedly threatening to kill him. Opening for the defense, Farrow countered that Schweiger was the one who was abusive. He had slapped Clara several times and even choked her and threw her against a wall once. In addition, Schweiger's relatives had looked down on Clara from the time she and Louis were first married because they did not think she was good enough for him, especially since she had been previously married. Clara longed for a child but was unable to have one of her own. They tentatively agreed to adopt a girl, but when they went to the orphanage, Louis favored Norman, and they ended up adopting him. Louis's relatives commented on the likeness between Norman and Louis, even though the boy was only seven months old, and this led Clara to suspect Louis might be the boy's biological father. Clara was brokenhearted to the point of melancholia when Louis divorced her and gained custody of Norman, even more so when her petition to have the divorce set aside was denied. The defense would plead temporary insanity on these grounds.[250]

In keeping with the prosecution's opening statement, most of its witnesses were called to establish that Clara had mistreated Louis, made unreasonable demands of him, acted insanely jealous any time he even spoke to another woman, and frequently threatened to kill him.[251]

For the defense, Clara's sister Anna Wallendorf testified that Clara habitually thought someone was trying to break into her house, that she carried a stick or some other weapon when she went around town, and that she exhibited other signs of paranoia. Anna thought her sister had been suffering from "a mild form of mania" for several years. The defense's case was hampered, however, when Judge Ralph Latshaw excluded certain testimony bearing on the question of Clara's sanity. For instance, one defense witness was prepared to testify that Louis Sweiger had told him he was divorcing his wife because she was "crazy," but the judge disallowed the testimony on the basis that it would prejudice the jury into accepting the defense's insanity plea when, in fact, it only went to show hysteria. "Hysteria is not insanity," Latshaw said.[252]

Almost as a counterpoint to the judge's ruling, the defendant broke down in sobs and cried several times during the trial, and one day the court session had to be cut short because of her "extremely nervous condition."[253]

Tiera Farrow gave a moving defense of her client in her closing argument, declaring that Clara's passionate love for an uncaring husband drove her to madness, but Farrow's pleas were to no avail. The jury got the case on Tuesday evening, March 7, and came back at noon the next day with a verdict finding Clara guilty of second-degree murder with a recommended sentence of fifteen years in prison. On hearing the verdict, Clara remained calm until she was out of the courtroom on her way back to her cell, when she started crying, screaming that she'd been convicted by lies, and begging to see her son.[254]

In early April, Latshaw denied Clara's motion for a new trial, but she was released on $10,000 bond, over the objections of Schweiger's relatives, pending her appeal to the Missouri Supreme Court. Shortly after her release, she sued to regain custody of ten-year-old Norman, who was staying with Schweiger's sister. The suit was initially denied, but she was granted the same visitation rights she'd had after the divorce. A few months later, she was granted full custody, pending the decision of the supreme court.[255]

On February 11, 1918, the Missouri high court affirmed Clara's guilty verdict, and she was taken into custody and lodged once again in the county jail. She was transferred to the state prison at Jefferson City on March 15, and she was paroled in December 1921, after serving less than four years of her fifteen-year term. In December 1925, on a petition from a large number of citizens of Jefferson City, where Clara was originally from and where she then lived, Governor Sam Baker granted her a full pardon, restoring her citizenship rights.[256]

10

"I SHOWED HIM THE ROAD"

THE STORY OF MARY APPLEBY

Sitting in a cell in November 1921 at the Greene County Jail a couple of days after gunning down her husband on Main Street in Springfield, twenty-four-year-old Mary Teague Appleby tried to express her feelings toward the man she'd killed in some crude lines of verse she wrote down on cheap note paper:

I gave him a lift, for he was my man;
I am bearing all the burdens I can
I gave him a smile when he was downcast and blue—
A smile that would help him to battle it through.

I gave him my hand, he was slipping downhill,
And the world, so he fancied, was using him ill.
I gave him kind words, I showed him the road;
I tried not to let him go on with the load.
For I know what it means to be losing the fight
When a lift just in time would set everything right.

I know what it means—just a clasp of the hand,
When a man has borne all that a man ought to stand.
Now I ask why it was with a quivering lip,
And a half suppressed sob while the scalding tears drip.

I was his wife in his trouble and need,
I offered to help him, but he didn't heed.

Written by Mrs. Mary E. Appleby, wife of Abe Appleby.

Although "critics might find many things to cavil at in the meter and verbiage of the lines," the *Springfield Leader* told its readers, "perhaps they express her feelings in the best way she knows. She apparently has but little education. And her recent years have not been devoted to the study of classics."[257]

The *Leader*'s last observation was a colossal understatement, because the only institution of higher learning at which Mary had matriculated was the school of hard knocks.

Mary was born in Christian County in 1898. The family moved to Stone County and later to Webb City, where her father worked in the surrounding zinc mines. In 1916, when she was eighteen, Mary married thirty-year-old Jim Thompson in Kansas City. They had a son, Edward, a year or so later, but the marriage was a rocky one. In late 1920 or very early 1921, the couple came to Springfield from Pittsburg, Kansas, and split up shortly after their arrival. Thompson took the boy and went to Rogersville, leaving Mary to fend for herself in Springfield.[258]

Mary became "intimately associated" with twenty-four-year-old Abe Appleby soon after Thompson left. Appleby was a ne'er-do-well who only worked "two or three days at a time now and then," and he depended on Mary to support him and keep up their home at 821 North Main. With Appleby acting almost as her pimp, Mary "played the hotels" in Springfield and gave Appleby most of the money she made.[259]

Her divorce from Thompson became final on September 17, 1921, and she and Appleby married two days later. Mary had to pawn a diamond ring and some clothes to get funds to pay for the wedding. Around the time of the marriage, Appleby sent Mary to Carthage to "work the hotels there." She got $200 from a man she met who was an old friend of hers and then called Abe to come and get her. On the way back to Springfield, Appleby "tore up the car," and Mary had to pay to have it fixed.[260]

On Friday, November 4, 1921, Appleby was arrested for allegedly beating Mary up, but the next day she put up his bail of $200 from money she had received a day or two earlier as a damage settlement after being struck by an automobile. Mary had recently received custody of her five-year-old son, but Thompson, on hearing of Appleby's arrest, came and took the boy back on Sunday while Mary was absent from the home.[261]

On Wednesday, November 9, Mary and her sister Eva Giles went shopping, as they later related the story. They were supposed to meet Appleby at the Portland Café at the corner of College and Main Streets at three thirty. When they didn't arrive until about four o'clock, Appleby, whom Eva thought had been drinking, grew angry at Mary for being late and started cussing her as the threesome walked east on College Street.[262]

They turned south on Campbell Street and paused at Water Street, where Abe demanded that Mary give him money to buy alcohol. Mary told him he didn't need it, and Appleby, who was carrying a .25-caliber automatic pistol, grabbed her by the arm and threatened to kill her. "I'm going to make you kill me," he said. "You've got to kill me, or I'll kill you."[263]

Mary said he could have the money if he would give her the pistol, and he complied, handing over the pistol when she gave him a dollar. The three went to a store on Main Street, where Appleby used the money to buy two bottles of Jamaica ginger. "Jake," as it was commonly called, was an alcohol-based patent medicine commonly consumed during the Prohibition era in place of liquor, and it was said to be a potent concoction that "destroyed the will and sanity" of those who drank it.[264]

While Appleby was in the store, Mary hailed a policeman she saw on the street and asked him to see if he could calm Abe down and make him treat her right, but the officer paid little attention.[265]

When Appleby came out of the store, he asked Mary to give him five dollars to hire a taxi. She gave him the money, and they caught a cab and rode aimlessly around town for a while.[266]

About five thirty, they headed back toward Main Street to retrieve some clothes that Appleby had left at a pressing store. On the way, Appleby said to the taxi driver, "Slim, here is a good woman, if you want her. When we get my coat, I am going to drop her in a dark alley."[267]

At the pressing store in the 200 block of Main, Mary exited the taxi with Appleby and tried to pour out what was left of the jake, but he stopped her. The two went into the store together, and Eva poured out the rest of the bottle while they were inside. When Mary and her husband came back out, he asked her to give back the gun he'd handed over to her. "You are crazy," Mary exclaimed. "I won't give you the gun."[268]

"Don't call me crazy," Appleby snarled as he started cursing his wife again.

Mary apologized, saying she "did not mean it the way he took it."[269]

Appleby was not pacified. He struck at her and grabbed her by the arm again. "This has gone far enough," he warned. "You've got to kill me or I'll kill you."

Mary fired the pistol twice, and one of the bullets struck her husband in his left breast just above the heart. He sank to the ground and died almost instantly.[270]

Two police officers quickly arrived on the scene and took Mary into custody. She was lodged in the Greene County Jail, where she was visited by a reporter from the *Springfield Missouri Republican* later the same evening. Described by the newspaperman as "slender, of medium height, and pretty," she calmly told her life story and related the events surrounding the shooting much as her sister later recounted them in court. "Her wistful face, grey eyes and golden hair," the reporter said, "give her more the appearance of a schoolgirl than an alleged murderess."[271]

After telling her story, Mary grew pensive. "God knows I've seen enough of men to detest them forever. But there was one man I loved," she declared, indicating that she was talking about Appleby. "He treated me good until the day of our marriage and then he changed."[272]

When a *Springfield Leader* reporter called on Mary the next morning, she related again the events leading up to the shooting and showed the bruises on her right arm as partial proof of her story. "I loved him, or I wouldn't have taken his abuse so long." She swore, though, that she didn't want to kill her husband. "I loved him," she repeated. "It was either him or me."[273]

On Thursday, November 10, the day after the shooting, a coroner's jury met and reached a verdict that Abe Appleby had come to his death by a gunshot from his wife, Mary Teague Appleby. On Saturday, a charge of second-degree murder was filed against her.[274]

Moved from municipal court to the criminal court to accommodate the large number of spectators, Mary's preliminary hearing was held on November 17 before an estimated crowd of at least five hundred. Most of the testimony tended to corroborate what Mary had said in the immediate aftermath of the shooting about her husband's threats and abusive behavior.[275]

For instance, Ellis Clifton, the taxi driver whom Appleby had called "Slim," testified that he heard Appleby threaten to kill his wife two or three times while he was driving them around town. He said that both Abe and Mary were drinking jake but that he never saw Mary's sister drink any. Just before the shooting, Clifton heard the couple exchange some angry words when they came out of the pressing store. The first sentence he understood was Mary telling her husband that he was crazy. "Then shoot me," Appleby snapped. "No, I don't want to shoot you," Mary replied. Appleby then stepped toward her with an oath and snarled, "Then don't tell me I'm crazy." Mary apologized, and the next thing Clifton knew, she opened fire.[276]

MARY APPLEBY IS HELD IN JAIL ON MURDER CHARGE

Woman to Be Tried in Criminal Court for Slaying Husband.

Headline announcing the indictment of Mary Appleby for the murder of her husband. *From the Springfield Leader.*

Despite the favorable defense testimony, Mary was returned to the county jail and held for trial in lieu of $4,000 bond. In early December, a grand jury indicted her on a charge of second-degree murder, superseding the previous information filed by the prosecutor.[277]

Mary's trial got underway in early January 1922. On the first day of testimony, "Never was the criminal court of Greene County more densely packed with spectators." One witness for the state testified that he heard a man's angry voice just before the shooting and turned in time to see the defendant pull a pistol from her pocket and fire twice. He said he did not see Appleby attempt to strike his wife, but he admitted on cross-examination that the deceased did have one hand raised at the time he was shot. An employee of the pressing shop said that when Mrs. Appleby accompanied her husband into the shop on the fateful day, she appeared to be in a bad mood, while Appleby did not seem to be angry.[278]

Seeking to make a case for self-defense, Mary's lawyers called witness after witness to testify that they had seen and heard Appleby abuse his wife in the days and hours leading up to the shooting. Eva Giles, the star defense witness, took the stand to relate in detail what happened from the time she and Mary met Appleby at the Portland Café until the tragedy unfolded in front of the pressing shop an hour and a half later. Testifying in her own defense, Mary repeated much the same story her sister had told.[279]

After two days of testimony, the jury got the case on the afternoon of January 5, and they came back a few hours later to report that they were hopelessly deadlocked, standing ten to two for acquittal. The judged declared a mistrial and dismissed the jury.[280]

Unable to raise bond money, Mary remained in the county jail awaiting her second trial. When the new trial began in early April 1922, spectators once again packed the courtroom. Mary's ex-husband, Jim Thompson, attended most of the proceedings, and Mary held their six-year-old son in her lap part of the time while the trial was going on. Testimony by both the state witnesses and the defense witnesses was similar to that given at the first trial. Several defense witnesses, for instance, said they'd seen Appleby whip his wife and threaten to kill her on the Friday evening prior to his death. Unlike at the first trial, Mary did not testify in her own defense.[281]

Testimony and arguments in the case ended at midafternoon on April 7, and the jury came back two and a half hours later with a verdict of not guilty. When the verdict was read, several of Mary's friends rushed up to offer their congratulations, but Mary herself took the news with "no undue display of emotion."[282]

Springfield authorities, though, hadn't heard the last of Mary Appleby. In late May, she was charged with disturbing the peace at a local hotel and fined twenty dollars.[283]

Mary soon moved to northeast Oklahoma, where her parents had relocated. She was married at least twice more after her move to Oklahoma, but she still wasn't ready to settle down. Mary was arrested on a charge of drunkenness in June 1929, and even the circumstances of her death suggest she'd never quite let go of the wild side of life. On February 15, 1941, she was found slumped over dead in Red and Lonnie's Taproom in Picher, Oklahoma.[284]

11

AN HONORABLE GIRL

THE STORY OF ADA LEE BIGGS

After twenty-year-old Ada Lee Biggs was convicted of second-degree murder in November 1928 in St. Francois County (MO) for killing her stepfather, William Simpson, newspapers speculated that the jury must have doubted her story because what she said at trial about Simpson sexually assaulting her on numerous occasions differed from the story she told when first arrested. While it's true that Ada's initial story didn't match the version she later told, if one reads between the lines, her claim of abuse at the hands of her stepfather was consistent with what she said from the beginning.[285]

As a *St. Louis Post-Dispatch* reporter observed less than forty-eight hours after the killing, the basic facts of the case were straightforward—on the evening of July 14, 1928, Ada poked a shotgun through a window of her home in Bismarck (MO) and blew the top of her stepfather's head off—but "back of the shooting [lay] a sinister tale of a middle-aged man, subject to brain storms and soaked consistently in Ozark 'white mule,' who was attracted by the daughter of the widow he married nine years ago, and who frequently threatened the stepdaughter's admirers with a .45-caliber revolver."[286]

Ada's father died when she was young, and her mother, Bertie, married William Simpson when Ada was about eleven. Simpson's inappropriate behavior began shortly after the marriage, as he first tried to kiss his stepdaughter when she was only twelve years old. "It's been the same ever since," she told the *Post-Dispatch* reporter. "I'm 19 now. If any young fellow looked at me, he would be crazy mad. He made my life a hell. It was just misery to me the way he went on."[287]

As Ada grew older and more physically mature, Simpson's advances became more insistent. He started groping her and trying to get her to go out into his car with him whenever her mother was away from home. Ada told her mother of Simpson's conduct, but Mrs. Simpson didn't believe her daughter and said she'd whip Ada if she said anything like that again.[288]

On December 15, 1926, when Ada was eighteen, Simpson, who was then about fifty years old, took Ada out into a car when her mother was not home and drove to a secluded road. When he made advances toward her, she flailed at him to fend him off and refused his order to get in the back seat, but he brandished a gun and threatened to "blow [her] damned head off" if she didn't obey. Forcing her to succumb to his will, he raped her. On the way back home, he threatened to kill Ada and "the whole damned family" if she told anybody.[289]

Ada left home after that and went to St. Louis to stay with Simpson's sister. In a matter of days, however, her mother sent word that Ada should come back home or else Simpson was going to have her committed to a home for delinquent girls.[290]

After Ada returned from St. Louis, Simpson's abuse resumed. He took her to the car and raped her about once or twice each month throughout 1927. He was so infatuated with her and so jealous of her that he would not let her go out with friends her own age. Simpson was given to "spells," during which he was mean to Bertie and other family members, and the Bismarck city marshal was called to the residence on several occasions to settle the man down. On Christmas Eve 1926, just after Ada got back from St. Louis, Simpson went on a rampage and started shooting a gun inside the house, firing seven bullets into the walls. Somewhere along the line, Bertie, forty-two, realized that Ada had been telling the truth about Simpson's abuse.[291]

Around August 1927, Bertie invited her thirty-three-year-old brother, Oscar Greenwalt, to come and live with her family in Bismarck to help protect her and Ada from Simpson. Simpson's spells worsened after Greenwalt arrived, and about the first of the year 1928, Bertie and her brother began plotting how to get rid of Simpson. When Ada was first let in on their plans, she shrank from the idea of murder, but as Simpson's spells and abuse continued, she grew more amenable to the idea.[292]

Simpson, who stayed drunk much of the time and was considered by neighbors to be about half insane, went on a daylong spree on Saturday,

July 14, 1928. About five o'clock in the afternoon, Bertie told her brother, according to their later confession, "We've got to do it today." Greenwalt agreed, and they appointed nineteen-year-old Ada to carry out the murder.[293]

Simpson suffered from ataxia, a condition usually resulting from brain damage that causes clumsiness and poor muscle control, and he took regular steam baths to combat its effects. The conspirators waited until later that evening when it was time for him to take his steam bath. Even at the last moment, Ada balked at the assignment she'd been given, but her mother took a shotgun from behind the door of her bedroom, placed a cartridge in it, and gave it to her brother, who cocked it and handed it to Ada. Then, Bertie and Greenwalt positioned Simpson's homemade sauna next to an outdoor window. While Simpson was taking a steam bath, Ada slipped up outside the window about ten o'clock and shot the man, almost blowing his head off. Bertie and Simpson's four young children were asleep in the house at the time, and Simpson's aged, blind mother was in an upstairs room.[294]

The shotgun blast aroused the whole neighborhood, and people flocked to the scene. Greenwalt called the city marshal, and he and his deputy arrived soon afterward. Ada, Bertie, and Greenwalt denied involvement in the crime, and it was assumed that some unknown outside party had fired the fatal shot. The lawmen arrested a young man named Richard Dennis on suspicion. He had previously courted Ada Biggs but had discontinued his attentions to her because of Simpson's objections. Dennis was questioned and released after Sheriff H.B. Watts arrived, as the young man was able to prove that he was elsewhere at the time of the murder. By the time bloodhounds were brought in, so many people had milled around the house that the dogs' efforts to track the killer proved futile.[295]

The sheriff and other lawmen continued to work the case throughout the night, and the next morning, July 15, Sheriff Watts discovered some shotgun shells by the fence in the Simpson yard, as if they'd been tossed there to dispose of them. The wadding in the shells exactly matched the wadding that had been found outside the window where Simpson had been shot. Based on this evidence, Greenwalt was arrested and taken to Elvins (now part of Park Hills) for questioning. Greenwalt soon confessed, implicating his sister and her daughter.[296]

Greenwalt was taken back to Bismarck to Justice C.H. Lucy. Ada was then arrested and brought there. She at first adamantly denied involvement in the murder, but she, too, soon confessed when confronted by Greenwalt.

Bertie Simpson was next arrested, and when told of her brother's and her daughter's confessions, she also admitted her part in the crime.[297]

Before leaving Lucy's office, Ada signed a full confession, which read as follows:

> *I, Ada Biggs, of lawful age, do solemnly swear that the following statements made by me are true.*
>
> *I am nineteen years of age and will be twenty years of age July 20, 1928. I live with my mother, Bertie Simpson; my stepfather, William Simpson; my uncle Richard Oscar Greenwalt, and my three little sisters and one little brother.*
>
> *My mother and I did not get along with my stepfather, and this condition had existed for about four or five years.*
>
> *My uncle came to live with us about eleven months ago and was working in the little shop out from the side of the house.*
>
> *My mother and uncle about seven months ago began telling me that, if we could get rid of my stepfather…we could have peace in the family and plenty. When they began talking this to me at first, I told them that I would not do anything like that. Nearly every time I went down to the shop, they, my mother and uncle, would tell me that something had to be done, and I always refused. They said something had to be done and wanted to know if I couldn't think of something to do, and I told them no, that I would get out of the way. About two or three weeks ago, they told me to kill him, and he would be out of the way. They said they would do all the work. In answer to this, I told them no, that I would not do anything like that. They kept on planning, and three or four days ago they said that they had all their plans fixed and would do all the work if I would just pull the trigger, and I said that is the wrong thing to do and I didn't think they ought to try anything like that. They just kept on, and last night, Saturday night, July 14, 1928, at about four or five o'clock, they, my mother and uncle Oscar, said when he gets in his sweat box, you pull the trigger and we will do all the rest, and I said, "Uncle Oscar, I don't want to do this," and he says, "Do this, and it will mean your freedom, for you know what he has done to you," and I said, "Well, I guess I can." That was all that was said or done until about ten o'clock, when my stepfather was in his sweat bath. When he got in his sweat bath, they said all right, now do your work. At this time, we were in the front room, and I went around to the side window where my stepfather was, and they made me take the gun around with me. Uncle Oscar handed me the gun, which was a double-barreled twelve-gauge*

shot gun and which was loaded, and he pulled the hammer back, and I went around to the window and fired the shot at my stepfather, and the shots took effect in the head.

They both told me that, if I would do that, they would get me a new car or anything that I wanted.

At the time I was at the window ready to fire the shot, my uncle was in the kitchen with my stepfather, and my mother was in the bedroom with the baby. After I fired the shot, I went back around to the front of the house. My mother was there, and I gave the gun to mother, and she took the gun and put it where it always sets, and they hollered for help. The reason for doing this was that my stepfather was mean to me, had threatened to kill me several times and would not let me have any pleasures, have either girl or boy company, and my life was a total wreck and misery to me the way it was.

I further state that this statement is not made because of any coercion, fear or restraint, nor have I been offered any immunities under the law of the state, but it is a purely voluntary statement on my part.

Ada Lee Biggs.

State of Missouri, County of St. Francois

Subscribed and sworn to before me this the 15th day of July, 1928.

C.H. Lucy, Notary Public.[298]

After the confession, Ada, her mother, and her uncle were taken to Farmington and lodged in the county jail. By the next day, July 16, Ada had already revealed more details about why she killed her stepfather. Not only had he tried to kiss her when she was just twelve years old and refused to let her have friends, but he had also made life hell for the whole family for many years. Even Simpson's own mother, according to Ada and her codefendants, cried out, after learning that he was dead, "He's in hell right now. He was so evil."[299]

Ada said that when she killed Simpson, she was thinking of "all the things Simpson had done to her" over the previous eight years and that she did not regret her actions. "I admit shooting him," she told the *Post-Dispatch* reporter, "but it was self-defense. I did it to free my family and myself, and I did it for the good of the community. I haven't anything to hide. I'll tell my whole story when I face the judge."[300]

Speaking to another St. Lous reporter the same day, Ada said even more about why she'd killed Simpson. "It was a case of self-defense for my pleasure," she said.

"What do you mean?" the reporter asked.

"He wouldn't let me go out or have any boy or girl friends. And then, last week, he brutally insulted me. He drew a pistol on me when I resisted. That's why I killed him."[301]

Simpson's mother, who was upstairs in the home when the shooting occurred, had a different story to tell the reporter. "I'd been expecting it," she said. "I heard them talking about killing my son and me seven months ago. You see, I own this house, and if they killed us both, then she (Mrs. Simpson) could bring her kinfolks here to live and they'd have a pretty good thing of it."[302]

Ada now claimed, a day after her initial confession, that she acted alone, and her mother and uncle accordingly denied any involvement in the crime. Greenwalt declined to say how it was that, if he had no involvement in the crime, he knew all the details of the shooting when he first confessed, even before authorities interviewed Ada. So, it seems likely that Ada was taking full blame for the crime to try to shield her mother and uncle.[303]

Regardless of the exact facts of the case, the people of Bismarck exhibited "a strong sentiment in favor of Ada" in the immediate aftermath of the shooting, while they were mostly indifferent toward Oscar Greenwalt and his sister.[304]

Ada Lee Biggs takes the stand to testify in her own defense. *Author's collection.*

Ada's case was severed from the other two defendants, and when her trial came up at Farmington in November 1928, she did, as she'd promised: told her whole story. Described as "five feet six inches tall, a bit chubby, with dark simply bobbed hair framing her round face," Ada calmly addressed the jury and her lawyers while holding back tears. Even when the prosecutors grilled her on cross-examination, "she was restrained and added a 'sir' to her responses."[305]

She testified about the various times Simpson had assaulted her, and then her lawyer asked how that made her feel. She faced the jury box and addressed the members of the jury in an even

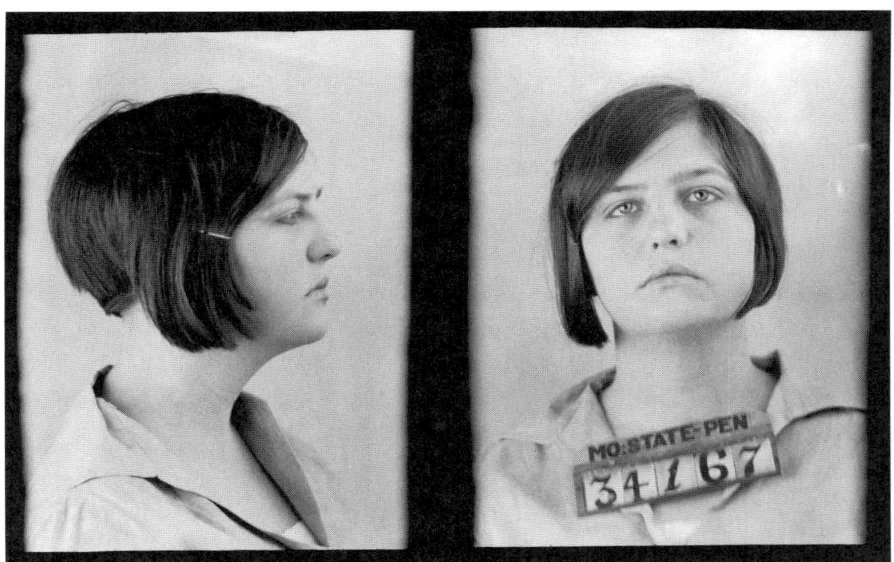

Ada Lee Biggs's mug shot. *Courtesy Missouri State Archives.*

voice, "Gentlemen of the jury, after I'd been driven to do this, after my honor, my virtue, had been taken, I realized I could never marry. My social standing, my character, were ruined. That is what drove me to the insanity that I did. If there had been any way out of the hell I was living, I would have taken it. He said he would follow me wherever I went and kill me."[306]

Over an objection from the defense, the prosecution was able to get Ada's initial confession entered into the record, and the prosecutors stressed that here at her trial was the first time Ada had mentioned a pattern of persistent abuse. The state also pointed out that Simpson was missing all four fingers from his right hand and suggested that he could not, therefore, have held a gun in his right hand and threatened Ada with it the way she said. Still on the stand, Ada pointed to her knuckles and said vehemently, "He had stubs as long as that." Her lawyers added that despite missing the four fingers, Simpson, who ran a garage, was considered one of the best mechanics for miles around.[307]

Two or three defense witnesses testified to Ada's good reputation prior to the crime, including Richard Dennis, the young man who had been briefly detained as a suspect after the shooting. He said that when he was keeping company with Ada, she was "an honorable girl."[308]

Although Ada had been charged with first-degree murder, the jury came back with a verdict finding her guilty of second-degree murder. So,

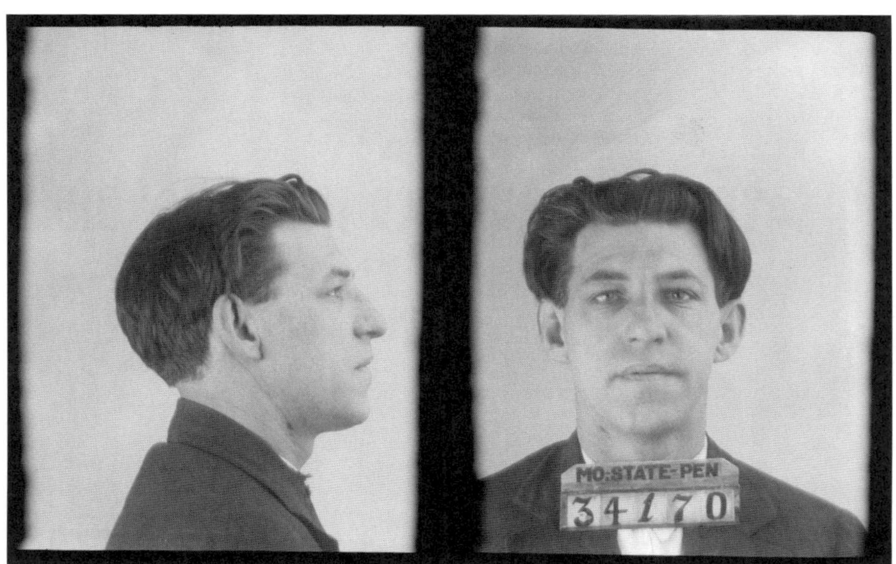

Oscar Greenwalt mug shot. *Courtesy Missouri State Archives.*

it is not clear, as the newspapers suggested, that the jury did not believe her story. It might well be that they did believe it but still felt obligated by the law to find her guilty of the lesser offense because of the cold-blooded nature of the killing.[309]

Arguing for the idea that many people did believe Ada's story is the fact that she was sentenced to only ten years in prison, while her mother and uncle, who both pleaded guilty to second-degree murder a couple of weeks after Ada's trial, received sentences of fifteen years behind bars. Ada was paroled in mid-1933, after serving less than five years, while Greenwalt and his sister were not released until 1936. Ada married the same year she was released, and the couple later had two children. She died in 1979 and is buried at Cape Girardeau.[310]

12

"I HAVE KILLED HIM AND I'M GLAD I DID"

THE STORY OF LACULIA CURRY

On the night of Wednesday, July 15, 1931, thirty-one-year-old Winston Edwards and his wife, Irene, came to the Deer Street Police Station in St. Louis about eleven thirty to lodge a complaint that a young woman named LaCulia Curry had been harassing them all afternoon and evening. Edwards, who was said to be a "highly respected man by his neighbors," reported that Curry had been hanging around the apartment building at 3749 Aldine Street where he and his wife lived and that she even threatened to shoot both of them at one point.[311]

Two beat officers were assigned to investigate Edwards's complaint, and they rode on the passenger-side running board of his Ford coupe as he drove them back toward his home, where he'd last seen Curry. As they approached the apartment building on Aldine Street, Edwards spotted Curry, pointed her out to the officers, and slowed to let them off. They started around the vehicle to question Curry, but before they could reach her, she whipped out a .38-caliber revolver, jumped on the driver's-side running board, and fired two shots at Edwards. One struck him in the chest and one in the hip, and he sank down in the seat.[312]

"You have shot him!" Irene cried out.

"Yes, I have killed him," LaCulia retorted, "and I am glad I did." She then turned the gun on herself and shot herself in the side, inflicting a serious wound.[313]

Edwards died almost instantly, but Curry was rushed to City Hospital No. 2, where she gave a statement before lapsing into unconsciousness. She said she had been associating with Edwards lately but that they'd recently gotten into a quarrel at the corner of Cook and Vandeventer and he had beaten her up. She showed off some bruises on her face to back up her claim. She said that she obtained the revolver after her fight with Edwards and went to his home.[314]

A coroner's inquest into Edwards's death was held on Friday, July 17. Irene Edwards testified that she had known LaCulia Curry for some time but did not know of any trouble between her husband and Curry. Irene said that LaCulia called her up and threatened her repeatedly on the day of the shooting and then came and loitered around the Edwards home all afternoon. It was also brought out during the inquest that LaCulia had thrown a brick through Winston Edwards's automobile some time before the shooting. At the end of the inquest, the coroner's jury ordered that Curry be held on a murder charge to await the action of a grand jury.[315]

LaCulia, who was employed as a maid at an exclusive women's clothing store, was still in the hospital eight days after the shooting, but she was well enough to sit up in bed.[316]

At Curry's trial in January 1932, defense testimony revealed that on the morning of July 13, 1931, two days before the shooting, Edwards and the defendant, who had been "keeping company" with each other, had gotten into a violent argument, just as LaCulia had claimed. LaCulia insisted on getting into his car, and Edwards was equally intent on keeping her out. He put her out by force, hitting her head on the door as he did so. Then, as he drove off, her clothes caught on the rear of the automobile and she was dragged a considerable distance, bruising her severely. Two days later, LaCulia armed herself and went to Edwards's home.[317]

LaCulia took the stand in her own defense but answered only two questions. She said she killed Edwards because she was afraid he'd kill her and she acted in self-defense. By restricting his questions to the issue of self-defense, LaCulia's attorney did not give the prosecution grounds for questioning her about her character or reputation for morality.[318]

One of the main prosecution witnesses was Irene Edwards. She said she was married to Winston Edwards for six years but that she had only learned of his affair with the Curry girl shortly before the shooting. Irene told of numerous phone calls she'd received from Curry in the days leading up to the shooting. In one of them, LaCulia allegedly said, "You've had him for six years, but he's been mine for four years."[319]

Charged with first-degree murder, LaCulia was found guilty of second-degree murder with a recommended sentence of ten years in the state

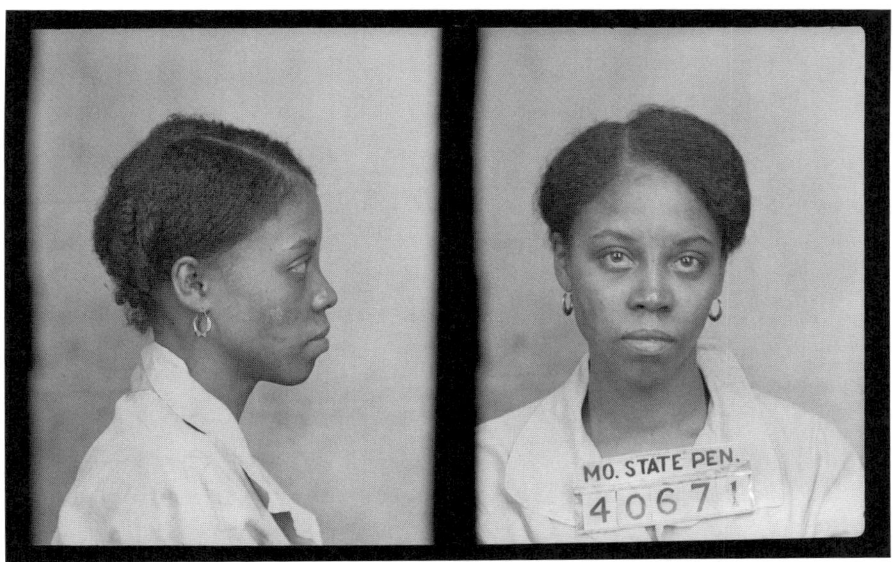

LaCulia Curry mug shot. *Courtesy Missouri State Archives.*

penitentiary. A few days after her conviction, while awaiting formal sentencing, she was interviewed in the St. Louis City Jail by a reporter for the *St. Louis Argus*, the city's Black-owned newspaper. "Still frail and showing signs of the strain of her trial," according to the reporter, "but apparently fully recovered from the bullet wound in her side…she seemed remorseful and ready to take her punishment."[320]

Expressing regret for the tragedy that had stained her life and even greater sorrow for the pain it had caused her mother, LaCulia said,

> *My mother is innocent of everything about the whole affair. If I had listened to her, I would have been at home this very day. She has begged me with tears in her eyes for the past two years to give Winston up. I thought I was past twenty-one and knew what I wanted to do, but to this day, I only regret that I never took her warning. My head was hard. I've made my bed hard, and I'm going to be a woman enough for her sake to sleep in it.*
>
> *For my part, life doesn't hold any interest whatever, for me; only for my mother and aunt.*
>
> *I worked for my living all my life. I started out at the age of twelve by scrubbing steps after school and on Saturdays. When I was sixteen, I quit school and worked at Sonnenfelds, Sensenbrenners, and the past six years*

> *I've been working at Steinbergs. I was converted four years ago at the First Baptist Church and was baptized by Rev. O.C. Maxwell.*
>
> *There were many untrue things said about my character and my mother, but thanks to God the majority of my friends know that they are false.*
>
> *I have been terribly mistreated by Winston, disgraced and abused. No one but God above and myself know. No one knows the whole inside story but myself; it would take up every page in the paper, but that has passed. And I am only trying to live for the future. God left me here to show the public that I can serve my time like a woman and also serve God better than I have in the past years. And sooner or later He will make my family happy again.*
>
> *Everyone makes mistakes, but God does not love ugly. That is why he has punished me and is giving me another chance. God is going to pull me through, although it will be hard to be away from my family.*
>
> *I only regret that I didn't die when I was in the cradle. My mother has always taught me things that were right, and the only time that I do cry is when I think how much sorrow and gray hair I have caused her. But she and my family have forgiven me, also God.*[321]

Shortly after her interview with the *Argus*, LaCulia was transported to Jefferson City to serve her sentence at the women's prison farm. She earned merit time while incarcerated, and after she'd served only half of her assessed ten years, her sentence was commuted in early March 1937 under the condition that she find employment and "not associate with persons of questionable character." LaCulia came back to St. Louis to live with her mother and aunt, and she did seemingly continue her good behavior. She married Matthew Alford and was a devoted wife to him until his death in December 1958. She later married again, and in 1967, Governor Warren Hearnes granted her a full pardon, restoring her rights of citizenship. LaCulia died in 1978 and is buried in Washington Park Cemetery in St. Louis.[322]

13

VIRGIL REECE TAKES THE GATE

THE STORY OF GERTRUDE LYTLE

Gertrude "Gertie" Lytle was a troubled young woman. Born Gertrude Graham to George Monroe Graham and his wife, Luella, in Kentucky about 1902, Gertie married John M. Lytle at the age of nineteen in Craighead County, Arkansas. The couple lived for a while at Blackwell, Arkansas, but the marriage soon failed. Gertie's mother had recently died, and Gertie was cast adrift.[323]

From Arkansas, Gertie made her way to Tulsa, Oklahoma, where she worked for a doctor for a while. Then she went to St. Louis and from there to Kansas City, where she worked as a milliner. Later, she went to work for the telephone company. Her divorce from Lytle was finalized while she was in Kansas City.[324]

In early 1930, Gertie came to St. Joseph, Missouri. On Friday evening, March 14, she checked into the Jerome Hotel under the name of Ethel Jones. The next day, the hotel manager found her in her room shortly before noon lying in bed unconscious. Nearby was bottle that had contained poison, and on a dresser was a note she had written to a Plattsburg (MO) man in which she threatened suicide. The note was signed "Tilda Bear."[325]

The young woman calling herself Ethel Jones or Tilda Bear was taken by ambulance to the Noyes-Baptist Hospital, where she remained unconscious for several hours. In the meantime, police identified her as Kansas City resident Tiddie Lytle. (Teddy or Tiddie was a nickname Gertrude used from time to time.)[326]

Gertie remained in the hospital for several days, regaining use of her arms and legs, and during her rehabilitation, she made the acquaintance of an elderly woman from Savannah, Missouri, who was recovering from a fractured hip. The lady told Gertie all about her hometown, and she "painted such an attractive picture of Savannah that Miss Lytle made up her mind to live there."[327]

One day, after getting directions to the town, Gertie left the hospital and caught a ride to the north edge of St. Joseph, where the driver dropped her off, and she started walking up Highway 71 toward Savannah. Still very weak from her hospital stay, she went but a short distance before collapsing. Someone called Andrew County Sheriff H.I. Holt, who picked Gertie up and took her into Savannah.[328]

She asked to stay at the county jail, but Holt instead got a room for her at a local hotel. The next day, Gertie ate dinner with Holt and his wife, and they made arrangements for her to stay with a neighbor family, the McCormicks, and to work as a housekeeper for her room and board.[329]

Gertie first met Virgil Reece the same day she went to stay with the McCormick family, and the two "were immediately attracted by each other." Thirty-eight years old and single at the time, Virgil was a World War I veteran and a prominent citizen of the Savannah community. He and Gertie had their first date that very evening, and they continued to see each on a regular basis for the next two years.[330]

Gertie also worked for and stayed with families other than the McCormicks when she lived in Savannah. For a while, she worked in the home of E.C. Breit, a local undertaker, and during the spring of 1932, she worked for Reece and his father, former presiding judge T.A. Reece, on the elder man's farm a few miles east of Savannah.[331]

She enjoyed living on the farm and spent a lot of time caring for and raising the family's chickens. She told friends that she and Virgil were planning to get married as soon he saved enough money to leave his father's place. Gertie, who had moved around a lot, even as a child, felt at home for maybe the first time in her life. She told people she'd found happiness in Savannah and never wanted to leave.[332]

But her dreamworld came crashing down when she learned in early June 1932 that Marie Thompson, an old friend of Virgil's, was coming back to Savannah from Tulsa. Gertie noticed that Virgil "showed considerable interest" in Thompson's return, and he became cold toward Gertie.[333]

Gertie was devastated by Virgil's loss of interest in her, but she put on a brave front. She told Virgil, "You can play around with those other girls, but when you give me the air, you're going to take the gate."[334]

Gertie left the Reece farm on June 16 and went back into Savannah to stay with the McCormicks, but she wasn't as carefree as she claimed. A week or so later, she went to the Breit home on a supposed social call and was told that the womenfolk were in the kitchen at the back of the house. From having previously worked for the Breits, Gertie knew the layout of the house well and knew where various items were kept. As she passed through a middle room on her way to the kitchen, she took a .32-caliber revolver belonging to Mr. Breit from a drawer and slipped it into her purse.[335]

Gertie Lytle. *From the St. Joseph News-Press.*

Marie Thompson arrived from Oklahoma around the same time as Gertie's visit to the Breit home, and the Thompson woman began keeping company with Virgil. Still pretending she didn't care, Gertie told Mrs. McCormick on Monday, June 27, "I don't care if Virgil doesn't love me anymore. I don't love him; don't think about it." Mrs. McCormick later recalled that Gertie seemed cheerful that day and showed no animosity toward Virgil.[336]

But that was just on the outside. On the inside, Gertie was seething with jealousy and anger. That evening, about dark, she called the Reece farm and talked to Virgil's father. She asked whether Virgil was there and whether he was coming to town. Judge Reece told her that Virgil had left, but he didn't know whether his son was coming to town. Gertie, though, had a pretty good idea where Virgil was and who he was with.[337]

About eight fifteen Monday evening, Virgil pulled up in front of J.C. Hoshor's drugstore on the north side of the Savannah square in his Chrysler roadster and parked. Sitting beside him in the passenger's seat was Marie Thompson. She began talking to William A. Wise, a neighbor of her parents, who was standing on the sidewalk.[338]

Wise glanced up and saw Gertie Lytle walk across the street from the courthouse lawn to the sidewalk not far from where he stood. She paused for a moment on the sidewalk and then stepped off and walked around to the driver's side of the roadster. When she was within about four feet of Virgil, she stopped, pulled a revolver from her purse, and pointed it at his head. "Oh, my God, girlie, don't do that!" Wise cried out just as she fired.[339]

Virgil's head jerked back, and he slumped against the car seat.

"Why'd you do that?" Wise demanded.

"Virgil knows," Gertie said, as she started walking away.

Night patrolman William Wright, who stood only about twenty feet from the Chrysler at the time of the shooting, stepped over, and Gertie calmly handed him the revolver, which was later identified as the one that had been taken from the Breit home. "I just killed Virgil," she announced. Later, she claimed that she had planned to kill herself, too, and would have done so if Wright hadn't been so close by and confiscated her weapon so quickly.[340]

Sheriff Holt, who was standing not far from Wright, took custody of Gertie, and she was taken to the Buchanan County Jail in St. Joseph, because the Andrew County Jail was under repair. Virgil Reece was rushed to Missouri Methodist Hospital in St. Joseph and then removed to St. Joseph's Hospital.[341]

Some bystanders had been exploding fireworks at the time of the shooting, and Thompson was unaware at first that Virgil, sitting beside her in driver's seat, had been shot. Escorted into the drugstore in a dazed state, she said she didn't know the woman who'd shot Virgil and she wanted to know her identity.[342]

That same night, Andrew County prosecutor Harry Latham questioned Gertie about the shooting. At first, she would say nothing about her motive beyond what she'd said in the immediate aftermath of the crime—that "Virgil knows" why she did it. Later, she explained that she and Virgil were planning to get married "as quick as Virgil could get his financial affairs straightened up and could leave the farm."

"I worked like a pup," she continued, "helping him save money and trying to get enough money to get married."[343]

Virgil died at the hospital in St. Joseph at eleven forty-five on Monday night, about three and a half hours after he'd been shot. A warrant charging Gertrude Lytle with first-degree murder was issued the next morning, June 28, at Savannah. Later Tuesday, when she was brought from the jail in St. Joseph to Savannah for arraignment before a justice of the peace, she waived preliminary examination.[344]

Her trial was held at Savannah in late November 1932 in front of a crowded courtroom audience. One of the key points of contention between the prosecution and the defense was whether Gertie acted from mere spite or from righteous indignation. The defense's case rested on convincing the jury that Reece's rejection of Gertie had driven her to temporary insanity. Although insinuations of intimacy between Gertie and Virgil were couched in euphemistic terms, implicit in the defense argument was that Reece had taken the defendant to bed under a promise of marriage and then jilted her when the next young woman came along. The defense's most direct plea in support of this premise came when Gertie took the stand and swore that she had been "wronged" by Reece while she was employed at his father's home. Two or three other defense witnesses testified that they'd heard Virgil mention his intention to marry Gertie. The prosecution, on the other hand, said Virgil had made no such promises and that Gertie had acted out of petty jealousy. Judge Reece, for instance, testified that he'd heard his son say on numerous occasions, including several times in the presence of Gertie, that he had no plans to marry anyone. Even two or three state witnesses, however, were forced to acknowledge on cross-examination that they'd often seen the defendant and the deceased together, usually two or three times a week, from the spring of 1930, when Gertie first arrived in Savannah, until the spring of 1932.[345]

After closing arguments, the judge gave instructions that left no room for an in-between verdict. Either Gertie was not guilty by reason of insanity or she was guilty of first-degree murder, which carried a penalty of either death or life imprisonment. On November 23, the jury came back hopelessly deadlocked after ten hours of deliberation. The vote reportedly stood eight to four in favor of acquittal from the beginning and did not change during successive ballots. The judge declared a mistrial and dismissed the jury.[346]

At Gertie's retrial in February 1933, despite the fact that the charge was reduced from first-degree murder to second-degree murder, the jury came back on the sixteenth with a verdict of not guilty after deliberating less than three hours. The jury held that Lytle was now sane but was insane at the time of the crime, and she walked out of the courtroom a free woman.[347]

Very little is known about Gertie's life after her acquittal, although a report in the *Savannah Reporter and Andrew County Democrat* ten years later indicates that she had recently married a man named Joseph Neelands in Kansas City and that they had moved to Colorado Springs, Colorado, where her father and two sisters lived.[348]

14

BONNIE PARKER

THE AUBURN-HAIRED BANDIT QUEEN

Bonnie Parker and Clyde Barrow, the notorious gangster couple of America's early 1930s, were both Texas natives, but they carried out several of their more noted exploits in Missouri. While there is no solid evidence that Bonnie ever killed anyone by her own hand, she was certainly an accomplice to many of Clyde's multitude of murders.

When the lawless duo first made their appearance in Missouri, they were little known outside their home state, but that would soon change.

Bonnie and Clyde drove from Texas to Carthage, Missouri, on Halloween 1932 and rendezvoused with Hollis Hale and Frank Hardy, two of Clyde's gangster buddies. They took rooms at a motor court in Carthage, and the men carried out a string of robberies and other minor crimes during the month of November.[349]

Clyde had his eye on a bigger target, though. Near the end of November, he sent Bonnie into nearby Oronogo to scout out the Farmers and Miners Bank there and bring back intelligence concerning the layout of the bank and the town. On the last day of the month, the three men, driving a Chevy sedan they had stolen in Carthage earlier that morning, went into Oronogo to rob the bank, while Bonnie waited for them about a mile and a quarter west of town in Clyde's powerful V-8 Ford coupe. The men got into a shooting match with the bank cashier, which aroused the town, and the robbers hurried out of the building with a little over one hundred dollars. They then had to run a gauntlet of lead from an impromptu posse of citizens who blasted away at their vehicle as they made their escape.[350]

They met up with Bonnie outside town, ditched the Chevy, and piled into the Ford V-8. Later, two local men reported having seen a young woman sitting in the Ford parked near the spot where the Chevy was found abandoned. They said that she was wearing a red hat, a blue dress, and a black jacket and that she appeared to be nervously moving around in the car as they passed. At least one report said the woman was still at the wheel when the Ford made its getaway.[351]

WOMAN DRIVES CAR IN ORONOGO BANK ROBBERY

Bandits Escape In Hail of Bullets from Towns-People

In the aftermath of the Oronogo holdup, there was considerable speculation in the regional press as to who the bold robbers were and where they'd come from, but the identity of the Oronogo crew would be learned only after later, more spectacular crimes had made the Barrow gang infamous.

After the Oronogo caper, Bonnie and Clyde split with Hardy and Hale, returned to Texas, and picked up a new partner, W.D. Jones, who, at sixteen years of age, already had a criminal record. After pulling off a few crimes in Texas, the threesome headed back to Missouri in January 1933.[352]

On the evening of January 26, they were scouting out the Shrine Mosque parking lot in downtown Springfield, looking for a car to steal because the battery was low in the Ford V-8 they were driving. Motorcycle cop Tom Persell spotted them and pulled them over on suspicion. The driver of the Ford, Clyde, hopped out and ordered Persell into the car at the point of a gun. Bonnie had been riding in the front seat between the two men when Persell first saw the gang, but by the time he pulled them over, she had climbed into the back seat. So, Persell slid into the front seat between Barrow and Jones.[353]

As Clyde sped away from the scene of the kidnapping, Persell glanced back and saw that the girl (i.e. Bonnie) had something in her hand, but he didn't realize until later that it was a .45 army automatic pistol. Clyde ordered Persell to pilot the gang out of town, and they came out on the northeast edge of Springfield and started east on Route 66 toward St. Louis. They went but a short distance before Clyde demanded to know whether there was a back way to Joplin. When Persell indicated that there was, Clyde, after telling Bonnie to consult a road map, turned around, drove

Opposite: This headline is misleading, since Bonnie did not drive the getaway car until Clyde and his sidekicks had already escaped a hail of bullets. *From the Jefferson City Post-Tribune.*

Right: Springfield motorcycle cop Tom Persell, who was kidnapped by Bonnie and Clyde. *Courtesy Rob Schroeder and the Springfield Police Museum.*

back to Highway 65, and headed north. After about a mile, he stopped and ordered the captive to get into the back seat beside Bonnie. The gang made Persell scrunch down, and Bonnie covered him with a blanket so the desperadoes could get gasoline without anyone seeing their captive. At the filling station, Bonnie held the pistol on Persell under the cover while the fuel was being pumped. Afterward, Clyde ordered the hostage to get back in the front seat, and Persell noticed a whole arsenal of weapons in the floorboard as he did so.[354]

Persell later described the girl he sat beside briefly as "red-haired and not the least bit beautiful. She weighed about 110 pounds, was freckled, as red-haired girls often are, and was wearing a dark coat and a sort of turban-like hat on the side of her head."[355]

About seven miles north of Springfield, Clyde turned west toward Pleasant Hope, and the gang took the back roads toward Joplin, skirting or passing through Morrisville, Greenfield, and other small towns. Clyde drove lickety-split over the rough, crooked, and muddy roads, doing fifty miles an hour much of the time. He kept telling Bonnie to look at the map to see which roads he should take.[356]

At first, Clyde was the only one of the three gang members who talked, and Persell thought he was "quite profane." But pretty soon W.D. and Bonnie joined in the conversation, and they were just as profane as Clyde. Persell noticed that Clyde didn't smoke, but Bonnie "simply ate fags." W.D. was also a heavy smoker, and he and Bonnie soon ran out of cigarettes and started bumming them from Persell. Clyde called Bonnie "Babe" or "Hon," and W.D. called her "Sis," while she called him "Bud."[357]

When the gangsters came out on Highway 71 north of Carthage, they seemed to recognize their surroundings and no longer had to rely on a map. They drove into Carthage looking for a car to steal but couldn't find one that was an easy target. Bonnie suggested they might find one in Webb City, and they headed there. Having no luck in Webb City, they drove to Oronogo, and Clyde remarked to Bonnie, "Hon, we know where there's a Buick here, don't we." Clyde then started joking about the holdup he'd pulled at the Oronogo bank two months earlier.[358]

Still unable to find a suitable car to steal, the gang drove to Joplin and tried to find one in the Roanoke neighborhood on the north side of town. W.D. got out and checked five different automobiles but couldn't start them. Bonnie saw a woman looking out the window of a nearby house and told her companions they needed to scram. "Hell, it won't be long until the law gets here," she swore.[359]

The gang drove back to Oronogo, where Clyde stole a battery from another vehicle and, with help from Persell and W.D., put it in the Ford V-8. A short time later, the gangsters let Persell out near Carl Junction with instructions on how to get to the nearest telephone. Showing more gumption than sense, Persell asked Clyde to return the gun he'd taken from him, and Clyde told him, "You're lucky as it is."[360]

Persell made his way to the outskirts of Joplin, where he called the Joplin police, who, in turn, notified the Springfield police, and they came and got him. Based on the story Persell told, authorities were pretty sure his kidnappers were members of the same gang that had robbed the Oronogo bank. They were right on that point, of course, but they mistakenly thought that the hoodlums must have been from around Joplin or Carthage because of their familiarity with the territory.[361]

After releasing Persell, the Barrow gang fled to Texas, where they hooked up with Clyde's brother, Buck, when he was released from prison in March 1933. With Buck and his wife, Blanche, in one car and Clyde, Bonnie, and W.D. in another, all five gang members drove back to Missouri and, under assumed names, rented an apartment about April 1, 1933, in the south part of Joplin with the intention of relaxing and laying low for a while.[362]

During the next few days, Bonnie and Blanche made trips to a local five-and-dime store to buy costume jewelry and other knickknacks, and they also purchased linens and blankets to fix up the apartment. Bonnie sometimes helped Blanche with the cooking, but she mostly passed the time writing poetry and playing cards. The Prohibition ban on beer sales was lifted about a week after the gang landed in Joplin, and Clyde, Buck, and Bonnie began going through a case of beer a day. The gang kept largely to themselves, but Bonnie found time to befriend a little girl who lived near the apartment.[363]

When the gang began running low on cash, the men pulled off a series of burglaries in the area. The nighttime comings and goings and the gang's other unusual behavior, like switching license plates on their vehicles, aroused suspicion among their neighbors. When W.D. stole a Ford roadster and Clyde let him bring it back to the apartment on April 12, Clyde and Bonnie got into a violent argument about it, because she thought it was stupid to bring another stolen vehicle back to the apartment if they were trying to be inconspicuous. Clyde, who didn't like being challenged, smacked Bonnie across the room, but according to Blanche's recollection, the gutsy Bonnie "got up and went back for more." Later, they made up, as they always did after a fight.[364]

Having received several tips about the gang holed up in south Joplin, local authorities figured they were dealing with bootleggers, and on April 13, five law officers in two separate cars made a raid on the south Joplin apartment. One police car cruised past the apartment and parked on the street, while another pulled directly into the apartment's driveway. As the three officers in the latter vehicle started to get out, one of the men inside the garage, likely Clyde, immediately opened fire, and a desperate shootout ensued. Upstairs in the apartment, which was located above the garage, Bonnie was recopying some poetry she'd previously scribbled down and Blanche was playing solitaire. Some reports claim that Bonnie picked up a gun and fired at the policemen from an upstairs window, but the preponderance of evidence suggests that she didn't fire a shot during the furious gunfight.[365]

Buck rushed up the stairway to tell the women they had to make a break for it, and all five gang members piled into their Ford V-8 parked inside the garage. The police car that had pulled into the driveway was blocking the Ford's path, so Clyde revved up the engine and rammed the obstructing vehicle, knocking it out of the way. The gang then sped from the scene, leaving one law officer dead and another mortally wounded. Meanwhile, W.D. was seriously but not gravely wounded, while Clyde and Buck suffered only minor injuries. One of the police bullets had struck a button on Clyde's shirt and barely penetrated his skin. Bonnie later dug the slug out with a hairpin.[366]

Left behind in the garage apartment were, among other items, some papers that helped establish the identity of the gang members, two undeveloped rolls of film, and some poems Bonnie had been working on. One of the poems, titled "Suicide Sal," was about a naïve young woman who fell in love with a slick-talking gangster. The *Joplin Globe* developed the film and published some of the photos in its April 15 edition. Several of the photos showed Bonnie in playful or provocative poses. One showed her smoking a cigar with a pistol in her right hand and her left leg hiked up on the bumper of an automobile. In another, she was pointing a shotgun at Clyde. Subsequently reprinted in newspapers and magazines throughout the country, the pictures quickly made Bonnie and Clyde household names and turned them into folk heroes.[367]

After the Joplin shootout, the Barrow gang again fled to Texas, where Bonnie was seriously injured in a car accident in June. The gang stayed on the run for the next month while Bonnie was on the mend and then landed back in Missouri in mid-July 1933. On the night of July 18, they checked into the Red Crown Cabins near Platte City, and their appearance and behavior quickly aroused suspicion. In the wee hours of the morning on July 20, law officers surrounded the cabins where

Left: This playful pose of Bonnie Parker was one of many photos developed from film left behind in the Joplin apartment. *Public domain.*

Right: Another staged photo—Bonnie playfully points a gun at Clyde. *Courtesy of the FBI.*

the gang was staying, but the desperadoes shot their way to freedom in a sensational gun battle that left Buck seriously wounded. Newspaper reports in the immediate aftermath of the shootout erroneously suggested that Bonnie and Blanche, "attired only in their nightgowns," had directly participated in the gunfight.[368]

In a shootout in Iowa a few days after the Platte City gunfight, Buck Barrow was seriously wounded again. Blanche was captured, and Buck died a few days later. The remaining three members of the gang fled west and then crisscrossed the country before dropping back down into Texas, where W.D. Jones left the gang and Henry Methvin and Raymond Hamilton, an old friend of Clyde's, joined it. Forming the latest iteration of the Barrow gang, Clyde, Bonnie, Methvin, and Hamilton headed north in early 1934 and once again landed in Missouri.[369]

On February 12, the gang stole a vehicle in Springfield and roared south with Clyde driving the stolen car and Bonnie, his "cigar-smoking gungirl," at his side, while Hamilton and Methvin manned the maroon Chevy sedan that the gang had driven into town. Abandoning the stolen vehicle between Galena and Reeds Spring when it overheated, the gang members piled into the maroon Chevy and resumed their flight with Clyde at the wheel. Just outside Reeds Spring, they encountered a roadblock set up by a local constable at an underpass. When Clyde turned around and drove back the other way, the constable gave chase, but the gang sprayed his vehicle with a fusillade of lead that forced him into a ditch. The gang turned onto a back road, where they came upon a local man, Joe Gunn, and forced him into the vehicle to guide them. Gunn noticed Bonnie, sitting in the front seat next to Clyde, holding a submachine gun across her lap. Coming out on a farm-to-market road between Cape Fair and Reeds Spring (now Highway 76), the gangsters again found their path blocked by law officers. They stopped, and Clyde, Methvin, and Hamilton got out and showered the cop car with bullets, with Clyde wielding the submachine gun. According to Gunn, Bonnie laughed with delight as her companions rained lead on the lawmen. When Clyde ran out of ammo, Bonnie, "his daring 'moll,'" reloaded the weapon for him. The two sides exchanged lead from about two hundred yards apart until the officers exhausted their ammunition. Then the men piled back into the bandit machine and roared past the lawmen.[370]

The gang let Gunn out unharmed near Berryville, Arkansas, and continued their flight toward Oklahoma. Gunn recalled his close call with the Barrow gang for a Springfield newspaper years later. He remembered that Bonnie "cursed a lot," and he embellished his tale by claiming that Bonnie had showered the lawmen's car with bullets as the Barrow gang made its escape.[371]

The Barrow gang made one last appearance in the Missouri region when they killed a town constable at Commerce, Oklahoma, just across the Missouri state line, and kidnapped the town's police chief on April 6, 1934. During the gang's pell-mell flight from Oklahoma into Kansas, Bonnie let it be known that she didn't smoke cigars, and she wanted the chief to set the press straight on that point. The law finally caught up with Bonnie and Clyde a month and a half later when officers shot them full of lead from ambush near Gibsland, Louisiana, on May 23.[372]

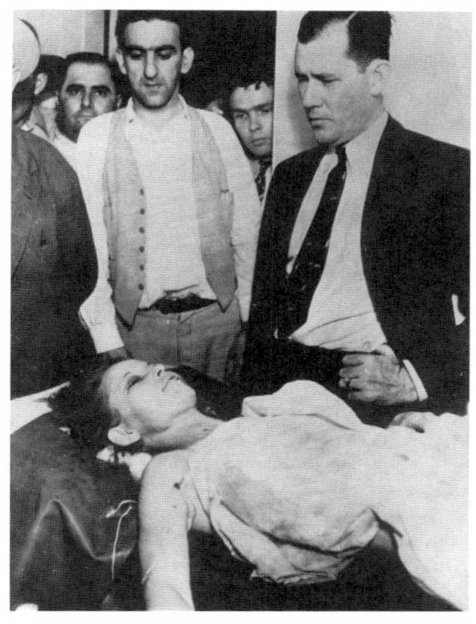

Bonnie Parker after she was killed in Louisiana. *Courtesy of the Jasper County Archives and Records Center.*

15

A TRIANGULAR LOVE TANGLE

THE STORY OF IMA GASKIN

After twenty-nine-year-old Ima Gaskin shot and killed Charles Spencer in her home at Hayti, Missouri, late on Friday afternoon, June 15, 1934, local constable Roy Wyrick was quickly summoned to the scene, and when he showed up, Ima handed over the revolver with which she said she'd accidently shot the man.[373]

During a coroner's inquest called at Hayti in the immediate aftermath of the shooting, Ima told her version of what had happened. A night watchman in Hayti, Spencer was a fifty-year-old widower and a close friend of her and her husband, Moreau Gaskin. He often visited in the Gaskin home, and Spencer called on her on Friday afternoon because she was in bed ill. Her testimony continued:

> *Talking to him in a joking way, I said: "People like you and me should be run out of town." He replied, "Or shot." Then he said, "Suppose we shoot each other—I'll shoot you first." I said, "Alright, go ahead."*
>
> *He removed his revolver from his holster, opened the cylinder and pulled out a hand full of cartridges. He snapped the trigger a few times, then pointed it at me and snapped it again. Then he handed the pistol to me, and I took it in my left hand, pointed it at him and snapped the trigger. The gun went off. He was just sitting down in a chair beside the bed after handing me the gun. After the bullet struck him, he slumped in the chair, saying: "Sweetheart, you've killed me but you didn't mean to." That was all he said before he died.*

The bullet, a soft-nosed .38 caliber, had entered Spencer's right eye, ripped through his brain, and lodged at the back of his head. Coroner J.W. Rhodes, who examined the body, said the track of the bullet would have caused almost instant paralysis and death and that the victim could not have spoken after he'd been shot, as Mrs. Gaskin testified. In addition, Constable Wyrick said that he did not believe the revolver Mrs. Gaskin turned over to him had been fired in several days. Contrary to what Mrs. Gaskin had said, he did not think Spencer had been killed with his own gun.

Three women who had been in the Gaskin home when Spencer was shot also testified at the inquest, but they were not in the same room where the shooting occurred and could not offer any pertinent information.

However, surprise witness Derondia "Dottie" Dunning, an attractive twenty-three-year-old woman who was separated from her husband, offered very pertinent testimony. She admitted to having an affair with the much-older Spencer during the previous month, and she told of a letter he had shown her when she was at his home the day before the shooting. The letter was from Ima Gaskin, and in it, Ima demanded that Spencer choose between her and Dunning. Ima wanted Spencer to come to her house the next afternoon, June 15, to discuss the situation, and she told him he was a coward if he didn't show up. Dunning said Spencer was very upset by the missive Mrs. Gaskin had sent him.[374]

On Friday evening, just a few hours after the shooting, the coroner's jury returned an open verdict, leaving the pursuit of charges in the case up to the prosecuting attorney and the victim's family. Constable Wyrick continued his investigation into the case that same evening. Spencer's son-in-law, in a search of Spencer's home, found not one, but two, incriminating letters and turned them over to Wyrick or another lawman. Both letters were from Spencer to Mrs. Gaskin, and both were signed "Love." The first letter was innocuous except for the familiar tone and intimate closing, but the second was the one Dunning had mentioned at the inquest, in which Ima demanded he come to see her or else be branded a coward.[375]

When Moreau Gaskin, waterworks engineer and street commissioner for the city of Hayti, was questioned about the apparent affair that had been going on between his wife and Charles Spencer, Gaskin, "vigorously denied the rumors, stating that his wife was not the sort of person to be involved in any scandal." The fifty-six-year-old Gaskin did not account for why, according to his young wife's own testimony, she and Spencer thought they were the type of people who should be run out of town or why Spencer had called Ima "sweetheart" after she shot him.[376]

Late Friday night, Wyrick arrested Mrs. Gaskin on a warrant charging her with murder, and she was taken to Caruthersville and lodged in the Pemiscot County Jail. She was brought back to Hayti on June 20 for a preliminary hearing before Justice Charles Morgan with an estimated three hundred spectators in attendance.[377]

Dunning repeated the testimony she'd given at the coroner's inquest, declaring that Spencer was visibly nervous about the letter he'd received from Mrs. Gaskin demanding that he come to her house. Dunning said Spencer told her he wouldn't go see Mrs. Gaskin except that he didn't like being called a coward. Testifying in her own defense, Ima repeated her story that the shooting was purely accidental, and she made light of the letters. She said they were sent in a joking way as comebacks to Spencer's accusation that she was having an affair with another man from Hayti. Moreau Gaskin, acting as his wife's counsel, urged the court to accept Ima's plea that the shooting was an accident. He "painted an unusual word picture of friendly familiarities existing between him, Spencer, and Mrs. Gaskin." However, Coroner Rhodes's damning testimony that Spencer could not possibly have spoken the words Mrs. Gaskin said he did after he'd been shot through the brain with a soft-nosed bullet and Constable Wyrick's opinion that Spencer was not shot with his own gun as Mrs. Gaskin claimed doomed the defense. After the hearing, Justice Morgan remanded Ima to the county jail on a first-degree murder charge to be held without bond.[378]

Ima's trial was held at Caruthersville in early August 1934. She came into court, according to the *Poplar Bluff Daily American Republic*, "wearing a freshly starched red and white checked summer dress, white strap pumps and grey hose," and "weighing 200 pounds or more."[379]

Prosecutor Robert Hawkins sought to prove that the killing was a premediated murder resulting from "a triangular love tangle." Ima had killed Spencer out of jealousy because he had become enamored of Dottie Dunning and was losing interest in Ima. Hawkins introduced into evidence the two letters found in Spencer's home after his death, and they were read to the jury. One letter began, "Hello, dear, how are you? If you like Dottie and would rather be with her, it's all right with me. Please choose between us as you can't divide your money between us and treat either of us fair, Love." The second letter read in part, "Damn liar…tell you just how dirty you are, you're fooling with the wrong duck now. If you don't come down here, you are a big coward. I want to talk over several things with you."[380]

As had been the case at the inquest and the preliminary hearing, the state's three main witnesses were again Coroner Rhodes, Constable Wyrick,

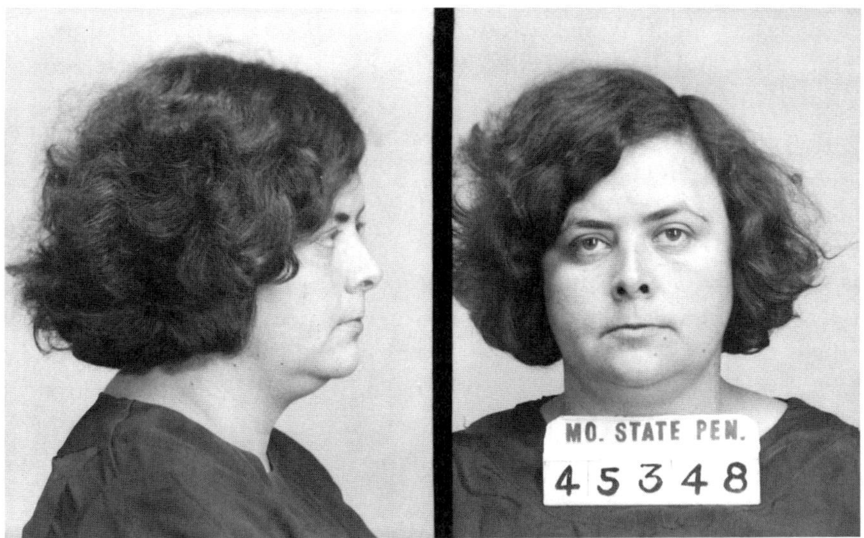

Ima Gaskin mug shot. *Courtesy Missouri State Archives.*

and Dottie Dunning. Each repeated virtually the same testimony they'd previously given.[381]

Moreau Gaskin took the stand in his wife's defense. He said that ever since Charles Spencer's wife died, Spencer had been a "good friend" of both him and his wife but nothing more than that. Gaskin denied that any sort of love affair existed between Spencer and Ima. Under cross-examination, he admitted that Spencer had been giving his wife money and that the payments had stopped once he became interested in Dottie Dunning, but Gaskin said no conclusion could be drawn from this, because Spencer and his wife had been close friends for ten years.[382]

Mrs. Gaskin also testified in her defense. She repeated her story of how the shooting, which she labeled accidental, came about. As for the two letters introduced by the prosecution, she said they were "just foolishness."[383]

Testimony and arguments in the case concluded about seven o'clock Friday night, August 10, and the jury came back four hours later with a verdict finding Ima guilty of second-degree murder and a sentence recommendation of twenty years in the state penitentiary. Her motion for a retrial was denied a month later, and she was transported to the state prison in early October. Ima's conduct during her incarceration was excellent, and she was discharged under parole in early January 1941 after serving a little over six years.[384]

16
THE MYSTERIOUS DEATH OF GROVER MYERS

When fifty-four-year-old Grover Myers died at Gravelton, Missouri, on April 15, 1939, after a two-week illness, the cause of death was generally thought to be pneumonia, and the people of Gravelton and the surrounding area mourned the passing of a well-known member of their community. Myers had lived in the vicinity all his life, except for a few years in North Carolina, and he had several siblings who also lived in the area, including Dr. O.A. Myers, one of the physicians who'd treated Grover prior to his death. Like his brother, Grover Myers was considered a prominent citizen, and he'd led an active life. As a young man, he taught school for one term and later became a contractor and builder. He had served as a justice of the peace, was a worker for the Democrat party, and had been a member of the Lutheran Church of Gravelton for several years. At the time of his death, he was foreman on a WPA project.[385]

A week or so after Myers's death, Edgar Bounds, a seventeen-year-old lad who had worked on the Myers farm, whispered that he'd once seen Myers's forty-four-year-old wife, Mary Louise, "in affectionate embrace" with Frank Stroup, a thirty-nine-year-old neighbor of the Myers family. This news set the neighbors' tongues wagging, and speculation soon arose that maybe there was more to Grover Myers's death than met the eye. If the neighbors had known more about Grover's time in North Carolina, their tongues might have started wagging even sooner.[386]

Sixteen years earlier, in June 1923, Grover and Louise, while married to previous spouses, had been convicted of "immoral conduct" in Guilford

County, North Carolina, on the grounds that they had deserted their respective families to live with each other. Grover Myers was sentenced to serve six months working on county roads, while Louise was sentenced to three months in the county home. Grover got his six-month work sentence suspended on payment of a $200 fine and a promise to return to his wife and small children.[387]

Grover Myers died in 1939 under mysterious circumstances of what was first thought to be pneumonia. *From the Fredericktown Democrat-News.*

He didn't keep his promise very long, though, because shortly after Louise's release, the two lovers got married at Winston-Salem, absconded to Missouri, and took up residence in St. Louis. After living in St. Louis about three years, the couple moved to Grover's home territory of Wayne County, and they'd been there ever since. But now, Grover lay dead, and rumors were starting to circulate in the neighborhood that he might not have died of natural causes.[388]

When Grover's sister Ala Whitener of neighboring Madison County got wind of the rumors, she began an investigation on her own. Already suspicious of the circumstances of her brother's death because he had appeared on the road to recovery the last time she'd visited him, she soon arrived at the conclusion that foul play was involved. Mrs. Whitener reported her findings to authorities, and Wayne County officials and Missouri State Highway patrolmen followed up on her lead. They, too, became convinced that Grover Myers had not died of natural causes. On May 4, the body was exhumed, a postmortem was held, and a sample of the viscera was sent to the highway patrol lab in Jefferson City.[389]

While awaiting a report from the lab, officers in Wayne County continued their inquiry into Myers's death, and Louise Myers and a second person were taken into custody on suspicion. Prosecuting attorney Roy McGee announced on Saturday, May 6, that the investigation might soon bring "startling revelations." McGee admitted that two people were being held for questioning, but no charges had been brought.[390]

Held at Ironton, Mrs. Myers adamantly denied any involvement in her husband's death until after the lab tests came back positive for arsenic poisoning late Saturday night. The next morning, she was taken to Fredericktown, seat of Madison County, where she was grilled by state troopers. Confronted with the lab evidence, she readily admitted poisoning her husband.[391]

Citing the fact that Grover "was mean to her" as the reason for the crime, Louise gave a detailed confession of how it came about. One day in early March, Mrs. Myers was visiting in the home of a neighbor woman, Nita Cook, and Frank Stroup was also present. Louise admitted to having been intimate with Stroup, and she said the three of them started discussing how mean Myers was to her. Nita Cook suggested to Louise that she should get rid of Grover, and Stroup seconded the idea.[392]

The three discussed the idea of getting rid of Myers a couple of times after that, and one day in mid-March when they were at the Myers home while Grover was away, Louise put a half teaspoonful of arsenate of lead into a bottle of tomato wine that Myers had made and that he occasionally drank. Louise claimed she acted partly at the suggestion of Stroup and Cook.[393]

Around March 29, Myers drank a glass full of the wine and became sick, but not enough to go to bed. A few days later, while still feeling

Prosecutor Roy McGee confronts Louise Myers with the bottle of poison she used to kill her husband. *Author's collection.*

ill, he drank another glass and started to the field to sow oats. After he left, Louise went to the Gravelton Post Office, and when she returned, Grover was in bed very sick. He asked her to call his brother, Dr. Myers. The doctor came that afternoon, and he thought Grover had the flu or pneumonia. Although Louise claimed her husband never drank more than two glasses of the poison wine, he gradually grew worse and died on April 15.[394]

In telling her story, Louise mentioned her arrest in North Carolina for living in adultery with Myers prior to their marriage. She also admitted that before that arrest, she had spent a brief stint in jail on a charge of prostitution. Louise said she had given birth to one child by her first husband and two illegitimate children, one of whom was born dead.[395]

She said her two living children were adopted by other families and that she had long ago lost contact with them. She said she had never been to school and could not read or write, except for her own name.[396]

After Louise's confession, she, Stroup, Cook, and Arley Kemp, another neighbor man with whom Louise was rumored to have been a "close friend," were officially arrested and charged with first-degree murder. Louise gave a second confession, but she denied that Kemp was involved in the crime. Authorities did not believe her, partly no doubt because Kemp had a previous criminal record.[397]

Law enforcement officers weren't the only ones who did not believe parts of Louise's story. Grover Myers's brother and sister, Dr. Myers and Mrs. Whitener, both said that Grover was feeling better and seemed on the road to recovery when they'd visited him just a day or so before he died. They were convinced that he'd been dosed with more poison after their departure.[398]

In late May and early June, Louise Myers and Frank Stroup were separately arraigned on first-degree murder charges, but the murder charges again Arley Kemp and Nita Cook were dropped for lack of evidence. Stroup was released on bond in July, while Myers was still held in the Wayne County Jail at Greenville.[399]

At the beginning of her trial in mid-August, Mrs. Myers repudiated her previous confessions, claiming that they'd been given under duress. However, the judge allowed the confessions into the record, and at the end of the state's case, Louise abruptly changed her plea from not guilty to guilty. She was then sentenced to life in the state penitentiary and transported to Jefferson City on August 17.[400]

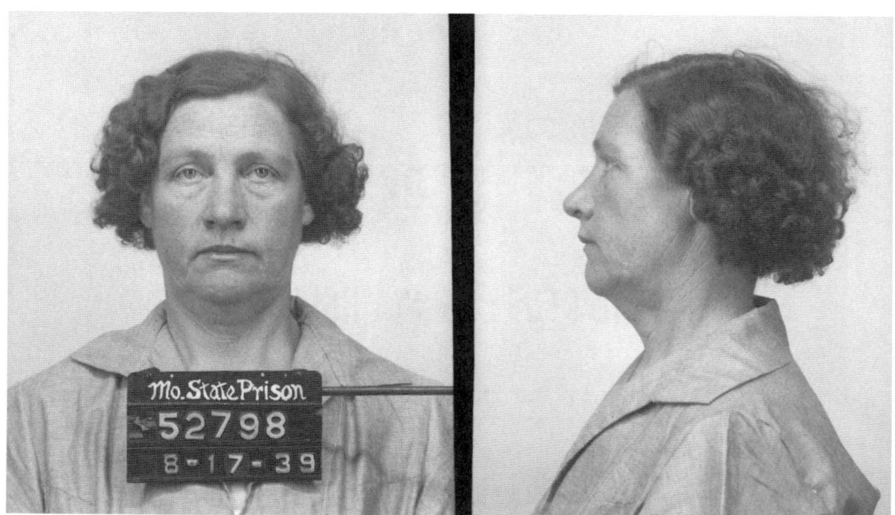

Mug shot of Louise Myers. *Courtesy of Missouri State Archives.*

Louise Myers was brought back to Greenville from Jefferson City to testify against Frank Stroup when his trial began in late September 1940. She repeated her claim that Stroup had urged her to poison her husband so that she and Stroup could get married. Stroup admitted an affair with the woman and even to being present when the idea of poisoning Myers arose, but he denied encouraging Louise to commit the crime. In early October, the jury acquitted him after deliberating for five hours, and Louise Myers was returned to the state prison. Citing her poor health, the Board of Probation and Parole paroled her in March 1952.[401]

17

SELF-DEFENSE OR MURDER?

THE STORY OF IVA HOLDEN

After twenty-three-year-old Iva Holden was charged with killing Max Lambert at her home near Bucyrus, Missouri, on August 20, 1963, she had a pretty good case for self-defense. The forty-five-year-old Lambert had been judged insane in probate court a number of years earlier, had been twice committed to mental institutions, and was known to have "bothered a lot of people" around Bucyrus in the past, including the Holden family.[402]

There were just a couple of annoying little details that belied Iva's claim of self-defense. The pathologist who autopsied Lambert's body said the man had been shot three times in the back, and the weapon Iva used was a single-shot .22-caliber rifle, which meant she'd had to reload between each shot.[403]

A World War II veteran, Lambert lived alone near the small community of Bucyrus, northwest of Houston on Highway 17, and his walking route from home to the Bucyrus store took him past the Holden residence, where Iva lived with her mother, Bessie.[404]

Lambert often stopped in at the Holden home on his way to or from the store, and he called there again about midafternoon on Tuesday, August 20, 1963. In the home at the time were Iva, her mother, and Iva's two small children. According to the story Iva and her mother later told, Lambert started "bothering" Iva and calling her "vile names." When he pushed her onto a couch, she got up and retrieved a loaded rifle that her boyfriend, Tommy Turner, had left in a closet at the Holden home. When Lambert started coming at her again, she shot him in the front shoulder. She then shot him twice more after he turned and started for the door.[405]

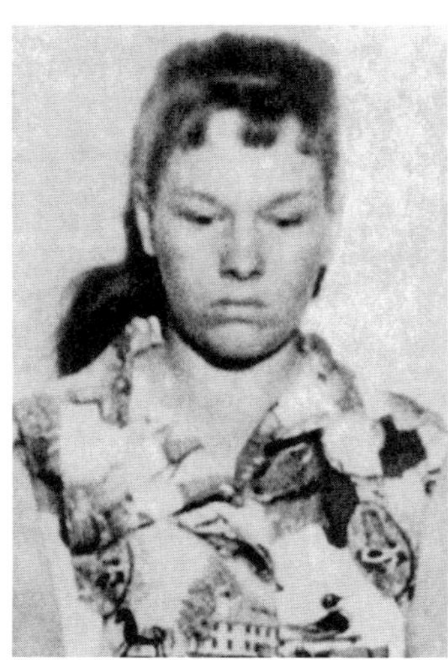

Newspaper photo of Iva Holden, taken shortly after her arrest. *From the Houston Herald.*

After a brief investigation, Texas County prosecutor John Alpers filed a charge of first-degree murder against Iva Holden on August 21. The next day, a coroner's inquest was held in Houston. The body had previously been sent to a Springfield pathologist for an autopsy, and Alpers testified that the pathologist had reported that Lambert was shot in the back three times. Alpers claimed Iva had told a story that "just couldn't possibly happen."[406]

Iva Holden did not testify at the inquest, but her mother did. Despite Bessie's claim that her daughter acted in self-defense, the coroner's jury ruled that Lambert had died from gunshot wounds fired by Miss Holden, and Iva was held without bond in the Texas County Jail.[407]

At Iva's preliminary hearing in mid-September, the courtroom crowd was "the largest in many years to attend a preliminary hearing" in Houston. Bessie again took the stand and testified that she and her family had often had trouble with Lambert in the past and that she and Iva had been forced to take refuge in the homes of their neighbors several times because of Lambert's threats. Based on prosecution testimony from the county sheriff and coroner, however, Iva was bound over for trial on a charge of first-degree murder. A certain level of sentiment in Iva's favor must have existed, though, because she was released on a bond of only $2,000, despite the serious charge against her.[408]

While out on bond, Iva got married to her boyfriend, Tommy Turner, who was also the father of her children. Then, in early February 1964, she went on trial at Houston for first-degree murder.[409]

The prosecution's two main witnesses were Dr. David Gorelick of Springfield, the pathologist who conducted the autopsy on Lambert's body, and Texas County Sheriff Len Wilson. Gorelick repeated his opinion that Lambert had been shot three times in the back. He also said he found no alcohol in the body and, therefore, did not think Lambert had been drinking at the time he was shot. The sheriff testified that when he first arrived at the Holden home after the shooting, Iva said, "I shot him." Wilson admitted on cross-examination that Iva had also told him that Lambert had come in and tried to throw her down on the couch. Iva's attorney tried to get Wilson to admit that she also told him of Lambert's previous threats, but the sheriff said he didn't remember that.[410]

Iva's lawyer opened the defense by exhibiting court records showing that Lambert had been adjudged insane in 1949 and had been sent to mental institutions two different times that year. He had not since been adjudged sane.[411]

Bessie Holden again testified on behalf of her daughter. Contrary to Dr. Gorelick's opinion that Lambert had not been drinking, Bessie said she smelled alcohol on his breath. She said Lambert, whom she and Iva had known for twelve years, came into the house without knocking and picked up Iva's youngest baby. "When he got rough with the child," Bessie said, Iva took the baby away from him. "He stomped and cussed and called us all kinds of names. He said he'd killed his mother and set her house afire and said, 'I am going to kill you'uns.'" (Lambert's mother had died in "a fire of undetermined origin" about three and half years earlier.) Lambert also threatened to kill a deputy sheriff and another man, according to Bessie.[412]

Continuing her testimony, Mrs. Holden said that Lambert grabbed Iva but that her daughter managed to free herself and went to the closet to get the rifle. Iva asked the man three times not to bother her. Bessie also spoke of an incident that had happened a few months before the shooting in which Lambert had twisted Iva's arm and threatened to kill both women.[413]

Unlike at the inquest and the preliminary hearing, Iva took the stand in her own defense. She said Lambert was coming toward her when she fired the first shot. Lambert then picked up a jug and raised his arm in a threatening manner. When Iva's mother knocked the jug out his hand, he whirled and struck the older woman. That's when Iva started firing again, but she didn't remember how many times she fired after Lambert struck her mother.[414]

After deliberating only thirty minutes, the jury came back on February 11 with a finding of guilty on a reduced charge of manslaughter and a recommended punishment of five years in prison. The jury obviously did not completely believe Iva's story of self-defense, or else they would have acquitted her. However, they must have had a certain level of sympathy for her, since she'd originally faced a first-degree murder charge.[415]

Iva was transferred to the state prison soon after her conviction, and she was paroled in early April 1965 after serving only a little over a year of her five-year sentence.[416]

18

FORTY YEARS BEHIND BARS FOR A CRIME SHE DIDN'T COMMIT?

On December 20, 2024, Missouri Governor Mike Parson commuted the life sentence that Patricia "Patty" Prewitt, seventy-five, had been serving for the alleged murder of her husband at their home near Holden, Missouri, on February 18, 1984. Patty walked out of the women's correctional facility at Vandalia, Missouri, in time for Christmas, but for Patty and her loved ones it was surely a bittersweet homecoming because she had served almost forty years behind bars for a crime she'd steadfastly maintained she didn't commit.[417]

Many people believed her claim, even from the very start, and in recent years, a number of groups and individuals, convinced of her innocence, had actively campaigned for her release. The prosecutors back in 1984 and 1985, however, seemed equally convinced of her guilt. Who was right?

Early Saturday morning, February 18, 1984, Patty drove with four of her children from her home north of Holden to a neighbor's house, where she called authorities and reported that her husband, thirty-five-year-old William "Bill" Prewitt, had been shot about three thirty that morning while he and Patty were asleep in bed. Patty said she was awakened by what sounded like a thunderclap to find an intruder standing over her. He grabbed her and pulled her out of bed onto the floor. She did not get a good look at the assailant because of the dark, but she felt a knife blade against her throat. Her attacker fled, however, when she started crying. Only then did she discover that her husband was still lying in bed—dead.[418]

Wife charged in slaying

Headline in a Kansas City newspaper announcing Patty Prewitt's indictment for the murder of her husband. *From the Kansas City Star.*

An autopsy performed Saturday afternoon revealed that Prewitt had been shot in the head with a small-caliber weapon, but the coroner said the bullet was too fragmented to determine the precise caliber. An initial investigation determined that the telephone wire to the Prewitt home had been cut, but no other signs of damage or a break-in were found. No weapon was found on the premises, but a .22-caliber rifle was missing from the home, while nothing else had apparently been taken. Patty Prewitt had superficial knife wounds "that barely broke the skin."[419]

The Missouri Rural Crime Squad, an investigative team composed of officers from surrounding police and sheriff's departments, soon joined the probe into Prewitt's death. On February 21, investigators found the missing rifle in a small pond on the Prewitt property.[420]

Patty Prewitt was arrested as a suspect in the case on February 22, but she was released into the custody of her attorney pending formal charges. She was rearrested on February 24 and charged with capital murder. She was then released again on $75,000 bond. Officers said they thought they had a motive for the crime, but they wouldn't reveal what it was. Shortly after her release on bond, Patty went back to running the family business in Holden.[421]

Patty's friends and family and the people around Holden were stunned by her arrest, and most of them could not believe she was guilty of the horrendous crime. Even Patty's father-in-law said he did not believe that she had killed his son. Patty and Bill seemed to be an all-American couple. They had been high school sweethearts while growing up in the Kansas City area and had attended college together at Central Missouri State in Warrensburg until Patty left school to rear a family. Eight years before the shooting, they had purchased a lumber and supply business in Holden and moved from Jackson County to the small Johnson County community about forty miles southeast of Kansas City. The Prewitts "liked Holden and Holden seemed to like them." They ran the lumber business together, and both became active in the community. Bill helped out with the summer baseball program, and Patty became active in her kids' school activities. She was also elected president of the Holden Chamber of Commerce.[422]

At Patty's preliminary hearing on April 6 in Warrensburg, the prosecution presented its case against her. A forensics expert testified that bullet fragments taken from the victim's body matched test firings from the weapon that was recovered from the Prewitt pond and that casts of boot prints found along the shore of the pond matched the prints of a pair of women's boots found at the Prewitt home. A Holden police officer said he'd seen Patty Prewitt wearing the boots on several occasions, and the Johnson County sheriff testified that the pond was later drained and additional boot prints were found leading out to where the rifle had been recovered in about eleven inches of water. In presenting the evidence, Johnson County prosecutor Tom Williams said, "It is inconceivable, indeed incredible, to believe an intruder, leaving a living witness, used Mrs. Prewitt's boots to take the weapon to the pond and then returned the boots to the house before vanishing forever."[423]

Patty's attorney countered that investigators had locked in on Patty as a suspect early on and had then looked for evidence to confirm their theory without considering alternatives. Just because her footprints were found along the shore of a pond on her property did not mean she had killed her husband.[424]

After the hearing, Patty Prewitt was bound over for trial on the capital murder charge and formally arraigned a couple of days later. She remained free on $75,000 bond.[425]

Patty was granted a change of venue to neighboring Pettis County, and her trial was set for mid-April 1985 in Sedalia. During the fourteen months since Bill Prewitt was killed, Patty had continued running the business in Holden, and her mother and other loved ones had stood by her. Bill Prewitt's father, though, who previously had thought his daughter-in-law did not kill Bill, was no longer certain. "We just don't know," Prewitt said.[426]

Earlier in the month, Bill Prewitt's body had been exhumed at the request of the prosecution, but officials would say only that they were seeking more evidence. When the trial got underway on April 16, Prosecutor Williams said the exhumation and reexamination of the corpse had revealed that Prewitt was shot twice in the head, whereas officials had concluded after the initial autopsy that a single bullet had fragmented.[427]

Williams said the state would show that Patty Prewitt had planned for several years to kill her husband, and her motives were "financial gain and sexual lust." According to the prosecution, she'd had at least three affairs, had offered one of her lovers part of the lumber business to kill her husband, and had offered another money. When none of them would take her up on the offer, she finally did the deed herself. According to Williams, Patty, in addition to wanting to free herself from the restrictive confines of matrimony, stood to gain financially from her husband's death because of a life insurance policy.[428]

Patty's attorney, Robert Beaird, admitted that his client and her husband had marital problems in the past, but he said their marriage had been on the mend in recent years. Beaird said he would call two of Patty's daughters as defense witnesses, who would testify that they heard an intruder in the basement of the Prewitt home on the night their father was killed.[429]

During the testimony phase of the trial, three of Patty's former lovers took the stand and claimed that Patty had offered them financial incentives to kill her husband. Testifying in her own defense, Patty admitted that she'd had affairs with four different men while she was married to Bill Prewitt but that none of the affairs had been in recent years, and she said the three men who claimed she'd offered them money to kill her husband were lying. "I never wished him dead," she said. "We needed him too much. The kids needed him too much."[430]

In closing arguments, Prosecutor Williams told the jury, "There is not one shred of evidence before you other than Mrs. Prewitt's testimony that refutes [the state's] view of the case." Beaird, Patty's lawyer, countered that the investigation was "shoddy" from the beginning, that officers had assumed Patty was guilty, and that authorities had pressured the state's witnesses into giving evidence against her. Beaird later said that additional evidence existed, such as testimony from a neighbor about a suspicious vehicle in the Prewitt neighborhood on the night of the murder, but it was not admitted.[431]

The jury returned a guilty verdict, and Patty was sentenced to life imprisonment with no chance of parole for fifty years. After the judge overruled a motion for a new trial, Beaird appealed the verdict, contending that certain evidence was withheld and that the instructions to the jury were improper. Patty remained free on bond pending the outcome of the appeal. In April 1986, the Western District Court of Appeals upheld the verdict and revoked the bond. Patty was transferred to the Renz Correctional Center near Jefferson City to begin serving her sentence.[432]

Patty Prewitt was released on parole after spending almost forty years behind bars. *Missouri Department of Corrections.*

Patty quickly gained a reputation as a model prisoner. While behind bars, she earned several academic diplomas, worked as a computer programmer for the state, and performed thousands of hours of community service. More importantly, she served as a counselor, a mentor and an inspiration to many of her fellow prisoners. "Despite her life sentence," said former Department of Corrections Director George Lombardi, "Patty has accomplished more, given more, and touched the lives of more individuals than many of us on the outside will ever achieve."[433]

Lombardi is just one of many people—justice system officials, lawmakers, religious leaders, journalists, family members, and fellow prisoners—who advocated for clemency in Patty's case over the past ten or fifteen years of her incarceration. Their efforts were finally rewarded when Governor Parson commuted Patty's sentence in December 2024. If one believes in the concept of clemency at all, even if you question Patty's claim of innocence, it's hard to fault the former governor's action in commuting her sentence. If anyone deserved clemency, it was Patty Prewitt.

19

"HONEY, EVE'S HERE"

THE STORY OF EVELYN SHIRE

The prosecution and the defense largely agreed on the events surrounding the Evelyn Shire murder case. In the wee hours of Sunday morning, August 7, 1988, Evelyn, forty-five, entered the home south of Lebanon, Missouri, where she and her estranged husband, John, had alternately been staying in recent weeks. When she found John, forty-six, in bed with his girlfriend, Judith Perryman, she shot him in the head with a .20-gauge shotgun. The only real question at Evelyn's trial sixteen months later was whether she was so emotionally distressed at the time as to constitute temporary insanity.[434]

John Shire had filed for divorce from Evelyn in October 1987, and he started dating Judith Perryman shortly afterward. The divorce decree was issued in July 1988, but Evelyn, upset that she was not awarded custody of her sixteen-year-old son or possession of the farmhouse where they had lived, appealed the divorce settlement. The divorce was, therefore, not finalized, and the couple was still legally married.[435]

At odds over terms of the divorce, Evelyn and John often argued in the weeks leading up to the shooting. Evelyn later said that John harassed her, mocked her, and sometimes beat her. She also claimed he tampered with her automobile and other personal belongings. All the while he was openly dating Judith Perryman and going out with mutual friends, which humiliated Evelyn and added to her mental anguish. At the time of the shooting, she was taking a tranquilizer, Librium.[436]

One of the things the estranged couple particularly argued about was possession of the house, located ten miles south of Lebanon on Highway HH, and they more or less took turns living there. Evelyn claimed she had been staying at the Shire home in early August 1988, but on the night of the sixth, John was there with Judith Perryman.

John said he wasn't feeling well, and he went to bed early. Later, Judith joined him. About three thirty in the morning, she was awakened by a light in the bedroom, and she recognized Evelyn Shire standing near the bed. "Honey, Eve's here," Judith told John, but before he could awaken, Evelyn shot him just beneath the nose with a shotgun blast that "massively fragmented" his skull, killing him instantly. Evelyn left, and Perryman, who was uninjured, called authorities. Evelyn was arrested about an hour later at her daughter's home in Lebanon.[437]

At her initial appearance on August 8, Evelyn was charged with first-degree murder and lodged in the Laclede County Jail at Lebanon in lieu of $300,000 bond. Laclede County prosecutor Jack Miller filed a motion to disqualify himself from serving as the state's attorney, because he had represented Evelyn in her divorce case, and a special prosecutor was appointed to argue the murder case. At the close of Evelyn's preliminary hearing in late October, she was bound over for trial on the murder charge and returned to jail in lieu of bond. She pleaded not guilty at her formal arraignment the following month.[438]

Evelyn Shire is escorted to the Laclede County Courthouse at the time of her trial. *From the Springfield News-Leader.*

Evelyn was transferred to the Greene County Jail because of overcrowded conditions in the Laclede County Jail. Her trial, originally scheduled for May 1989, was postponed so that she could undergo a court-ordered mental examination.[439]

The evaluation found she was mentally fit to stand trial, and the proceeding began at Lebanon in early December 1989. On the eve of the trial, Evelyn's attorney, Dee Wampler, indicated that he would seek an acquittal based on temporary insanity, while the state's attorney, Kenny Hulshof, who'd originally declared his intention to seek the death penalty, said he would ask instead for a sentence of life imprisonment without parole.[440]

Testifying for the prosecution, Judith Perryman said she was asleep in bed beside John Shire when the click of a light switch in the hallway awakened her. She saw Evelyn Shire standing in the hallway and saw her enter the bedroom and walk to the side of the bed. "Honey, Eve's here," she said to Shire. At almost the same instant, Evelyn placed the barrel of a shotgun within a few inches of Shire's nose and fired. Shire died instantly, and Evelyn turned and left.[441]

Evelyn took the stand in her own defense and said she'd been living at the rural Laclede County home alone at the time of the shooting. When she walked into the house, she found her estranged husband in bed nude and was surprised to see Judith Perryman lying beside him. After that, she claimed not to know what happened. All she remembered was "being in a dark hallway and hearing a lot of screaming."[442]

A psychiatrist who had examined Evelyn also testified for the defense. He said she was unaware of what she was doing when she shot John Shire and that she was now suffering from amnesia and did not remember the shooting.[443]

The jury deliberated for three hours before reaching a compromise verdict. They found Evelyn guilty of second-degree murder and recommended a sentence of life imprisonment but with the possibility of parole.[444]

Evelyn later obtained new representation and appealed the verdict on several grounds. One basis for the appeal was that one of the members of the venire should have been excluded from the jury because she was a friend of Judith Perryman and the court had erred in overruling the defense's challenge. Another point of the appeal was that Evelyn's diary should have been admitted into evidence to help show her fragile mental state. Another basis was that two witnesses who could have testified to the abuse Evelyn had suffered at the hands of John Shire should have been called but were not. Discounting each of the arguments, Division Two of the Southern District of the Missouri Court of Appeals upheld the verdict in 1993. In relation to the third point, for instance, the appeals court said that other defense witnesses offered the same testimony that the missing witnesses would have given and that Evelyn's trial attorney had chosen not to call them for no inappropriate reason.[445]

20

"I WON'T TAKE THAT ANYMORE"

DEBRA CARSON AND THE BATTERED WOMAN SYNDROME

Forty-seven-year-old Bobby Dean Hibbs had physically and emotionally abused his live-in girlfriend, Debra J. Carson, throughout their sixteen-month relationship, but when he called her a whore during an altercation near Allendale, Missouri, on Monday night, July 10, 1989, twenty-eight-year-old Debra had had enough. Facing Hibbs in the road outside their rural Worth County home, she fired at least four shots from a .22-caliber rifle, striking him once in the upper right arm and once in middle of the chest. The latter shot entered his heart, and he died soon thereafter.[446]

According to later testimony, Hibbs and Carson had been together most of the afternoon on the day of the shooting. Hibbs had been drinking and was intoxicated by nightfall. He and Carson had been hunting from a pickup truck using a .22 rifle. Around ten o'clock, they got into an argument in the road in front of the farmhouse they'd recently rented southeast of Allendale, and Hibbs accused Carson of being unfaithful. During the quarrel, Hibbs starting choking and striking Carson, but she broke free, ran to the pickup, and retrieved the rifle. After threatening Hibbs with the gun, Carson and her eight-year-old daughter, Julia, who was with the couple when the fight broke out, starting walking up the road away from him. When he came running after them, Carson told him to stop and fired a warning shot into the air, and Hibbs fell to his knees. "Don't shoot me, please," he allegedly said. "I love you, but you are a whore."[447]

"I won't take that anymore," Carson snapped as she opened fire with the semiautomatic rifle. One of the shots struck Hibbs in the chest, and he collapsed and rolled to the side of the road.[448]

Carson grabbed her daughter, and they ran into a travel trailer beside the farmhouse, then hopped in the pickup and drove to a neighbor's house, from where authorities were summoned. Hibbs was lying dead at the side of the road when officers arrived. Debra Carson was arrested and taken to the Gentry County Jail in Albany.[449]

On Wednesday, July 12, Debra was taken to Grant City, the seat of Worth County, and formally charged with first-degree murder. She was then released on $50,000 bond. Shortly afterward, she moved to Kansas City.[450]

There in early August, she told her story to a newspaperman, who described her relationship with Hobbs as "punctuated by bizarre sexual and religious experiences, heavy drinking and savage beatings."[451]

Despite the abuse, Debra said, "I still love Bobby. I don't mean to cut him down. I'll always love him."

However, she didn't feel as if she should have been charged with anything other than self-defense.

Debra said she dropped out of school after seventh grade, married when she was just fifteen, and divorced at nineteen. She had a baby and lived with a second man who "used to kick me in the ribs and all." Then she lived for a while with a fifty-eight-year-old man who later served time on sex-related charges.[452]

Debra was unemployed and had no marketable skills, but she liked to sing in country-music bars. In early 1988, she met Bobby Hibbs, a part-time carpet installer who enjoyed hunting and fishing, and they soon started living together. The relationship was turbulent from the start. Bobby "wasn't all in his head," Debra explained.

At first, they lived in Kansas City, and then they moved to Oklahoma. While there, Debra left Bobby when "he started drinking a case of beer at a sitting." He called her up, begging her to come back, and she did. They then returned to Missouri and went to Worth County, where Hibbs was originally from. They lived in a travel trailer next to the rural Allendale farmhouse, which they were fixing up to live in.[453]

Hibbs owned the couple's only vehicle, and he controlled their money, including Debra's welfare checks. One time, according to Debra, they went to Kansas City to get her welfare check, and she slipped out the back door of the welfare office to try to get to the bank and cash it before Hibbs could get his hands on the money, but he intercepted her and took the money. Debra said she was scared of Hibbs most of the time, but she was also in love with him.

Hibbs became especially abusive when drinking. "He'd call me a whore, say I was running around on him, say I reminded him of his ex-girlfriend, stuff like that," Debra said. "He was insanely jealous."[454]

One time in 1988, Hibbs made Debra strip naked and then beat her with a belt. He later told her it wasn't a beating since he hadn't hit her with his hands. Hibbs was arrested and convicted of abuse for that incident, but he and Debra soon got back together after he was placed on probation.

According to Debra, she and Hibbs had good days as well as bad. They enjoyed fishing and drinking together, but Hibbs sometimes acted weird. "He said he'd heard from God," Debra explained, "told me one night he thought he saw Jesus out in the front yard, slept with a Bible under his pillow." At the same time that he was having his religious hallucinations, though, he rented pornographic movies and wanted to engage in "unusual sexual activities," sometimes involving third parties. Hibbs kept a stash of weapons, including guns, knives, and bows, hidden in the trailer.[455]

On the day of the shooting, Hibbs had been drinking beer, ripping through a twelve-pack. At his suggestion, he and Debra got in the pickup and went "road-hunting." He killed a couple of rabbits, and they stopped for another twelve-pack. And then, Debra recalled, "Bobby suddenly wasn't Bobby that night. He started beating me, choking me, yelling into the night." He was stomping around and kicking at the ground and at the truck.

He briefly settled down, but then he started up again, lashing out at Debra and her daughter. Debra said she realized she needed to get out of there. She grabbed the rifle out of the pickup, took her daughter by the hand, and started down the road. Hibbs yelled that they couldn't go anywhere with his gun and began chasing after them. Debra tried to get her and Julia over or through a barbed-wire fence but had trouble getting across, and when she turned around, Hibbs was closing in on them, yelling and screaming. "I remember firing once into the air, hoping he'd stop. And then I saw him reaching down for a rock, and I fired at him." She didn't remember how many times she shot.[456]

She then took Julia's hand, raced back to the trailer, jumped in the truck, drove to a neighbor's place about a mile away, and yelled for help. The neighbor, Gwen Glenn, remembered that Debra was hysterical when she came to her place. She said she'd "shot her man, or her boyfriend, something like that."

Debra said she didn't own a gun and didn't know how to use one, "but I knew he was going to hurt me and Julia, and I protected my kid."

Worth County Sheriff Lorace Waldeier admitted that abuse probably played a part in the shooting. He said Debra had bruises around her neck and her face was swollen when she was arrested, and she told him at the time that Hibbs had beaten her in a drunken rage. Waldeier said Carson had given his officers no problems during the two days she'd been in their custody.

At the time of Debra's interview with the Kansas City reporter, some women's groups were already involved in her case, advocating on her behalf. Referring to the first-degree murder charge against Debra, a spokeswoman for a women's self-help group in St. Louis said, "I'm just sick about it. There's background information that points to a history of beatings, and she was hurt by him that night when she killed him." Debra's case fit the "all-too-familiar pattern" of a woman getting into an abusive relationship and having difficulty getting out. "We see this a lot, and then we see a legal system that can't understand it all and wants to take it out on the woman."[457]

At her formal arraignment in November 1989, Debra pleaded not guilty, and the judge granted her attorney's request that she be evaluated to determine her mental capacity.[458]

While still out on bond awaiting trial, Debra got married to a man named Lewis. The charge against her was reduced to second-degree murder, and her trial came up at Grant City in September 1990.[459]

The prosecution called half a dozen witnesses on the first day of testimony, but the main one was Debra's daughter, Julia. The girl described what happened on the night of the shooting much as her mother had related it to the Kansas City reporter. The prosecutor got her to admit that she thought the keys were in the ignition of the pickup when her mother went for the rifle, presumably trying to plant the idea that Debra could have gotten Julia and fled in the vehicle instead of retrieving the weapon. On cross-examination, however, Julia corrected herself to say she didn't think the keys were in the ignition.[460]

When it came time for the defense to present its case, a whole parade of witnesses took the stand to testify to the abuse Debra had suffered at the hands of Bobby Hibbs. In addition, Marilyn Hutchinson, a Kansas City psychologist who conducted an in-depth evaluation of the defendant, testified that Debra suffered from "battered woman syndrome" when she shot Hibbs. She exhibited a pattern of behavior that included "learned helplessness" and "traumatic bonding," in which a victim becomes

Battered woman innocent of murder

Newspaper headline announcing the not guilty verdict in the Debra Carson murder case. *From the St. Joseph News-Press.*

thankful when the abusive person stops beating them rather than being mad at the person.[461]

Taking the stand in her own defense, Debra said she acted out of an instinct to protect herself and her daughter when she shot Bobby Hibbs. She said she had no intention of killing him but that she feared more beatings if she didn't act. "All I wanted to do is leave," she said.[462]

The prosecution called two or three rebuttal witnesses to refute the defense's portrayal of Hibbs as a violent man who often beat Debra. Hibbs's sister said she never saw the couple fighting, and she blamed whatever problems they might have had on Debra's preference for partying over the quiet life that her brother preferred. Another rebuttal witness, Ethyl Parrick, said that, about a month before the shooting, she heard Debra say she was going to kill Hibbs if he ever hit her again. Parrick also claimed Debra had bragged to several people after the shooting that she was going "to walk," meaning she was going to be found not guilty.[463]

Debra Carson (a.k.a. Lewis) may not have been a prophet, but her prediction that she'd walk proved accurate. In late September, the jury, after deliberating for four hours, found her innocent on the grounds that she acted in self-defense. Marilyn Hutchinson, the Kansas City psychologist, said she was pleased by the verdict. "I'm happy for Debbie. I'm convinced she shot him because she felt no other possibility of an out at the time." Still, Hutchinson lamented the fact that women across the country who kill abusive partners in self-defense are, more often than not, found guilty of murder and put in prison.[464]

NOTES

Abbreviations for newspapers and frequently cited sources:

BRC	*Bethany Republican-Clipper*	*OT*	*Oakland (CA) Tribune*
BCN	*Blytheville (AR) Courier News*	*PBDAR*	*Poplar Bluff Daily American Republic*
CDA	*Caruthersville Democrat-Argus*	*SRACD*	*Savannah Reporter and Andrew County Democrat*
FN	*Farmington News*	*SJ*	*Shreveport Journal*
FDN	*Fredericktown Democrat News*	*SDN*	*Springfield Daily News*
GSCNO	*Galena Stone County News-Oracle*	*SL*	*Springfield Leader*
GNR	*Greensboro (NC) News and Record*	*SLP*	*Springfield Leader and Press*
GS	*Greenville (MO) Sun*	*SMR*	*Springfield Missouri Republican*
HMH	*Hayti Missouri Herald*	*SNL*	*Springfield News-Leader*
HH	*Houston Herald*	*SP*	*Springfield Press*
JCDSJ	*Jefferson City Daily State Journal*	*SJG*	*St. Joseph Gazette*
JCT	*Jefferson City Tribune*	*SJNP*	*St. Joseph News-Press*
JG	*Joplin Globe*	*SJNPG*	*St. Joseph News-Press/Gazette*
JNH	*Joplin News-Herald*	*SLDMD*	*St. Louis Daily Missouri Democrat*
KCC	*Kansas City Call*	*SLGD*	*St. Louis Globe-Democrat*
KCJ	*Kansas City Journal*	*SLPD*	*St. Louis Post-Dispatch*
KCP	*Kansas City Post*	*SLR*	*St. Louis Republican*
KCS	*Kansas City Star*	*SLST*	*St. Louis Star and Tribune*
KCT	*Kansas City Times*	*TT*	*Tulsa Tribune*
MNR	*Miami (OK) News-Record*	*WB*	*Warrenton Banner*
MSPD	Missouri State Penitentiary Database		

1. You Poke Me and I'll Poke You: The Story of Mary Ball

1. *SLDMD*, January 26, 1868; *SLDMD*, December 13, 1867.
2. *SLDMD*, December 22, 1867.
3. *SLDMD*, December 22, 1867.
4. *SLDMD*, January 4, 1868.
5. *SLDMD*, January 4, 1868; *SLDMD*, January 21, 1868; *SLDMD*, January 4, 1868.
6. *SLDMD*, January 4, 1868.
7. *SLDMD*, January 4, 1868.
8. *SLDMD*, January 4, 1868.
9. *SLDMD*, January 4, 1868.
10. *SLDMD*, January 21, 1868; *SLDMD*, January 24, 1868; *SLDMD*, January 26, 1868.
11. *SLDMD*, April 3, 1868; *SLDMD*, September 9, 1868; *SLDMD*, October 1, 1868; Mary Ball, Pardons and Commutations, Box 31, Folder 8.

2. Unlawfully Intimate: The Story of Martha Taylor

12. *SLR*, September 1, 1876.
13. *SLR*, September 1, 1876; *JCDSJ*, July 30, 1876; *SLPD*, January 18, 1877; U.S. Census, 1870.
14. *SLR*, September 1, 1876.
15. *SLPD*, January 18, 1877.
16. *SLPD*, January 18, 1877.
17. *SLR*, August 11, 1876; *SLPD*, January 18, 1877.
18 *SLR*, August 11, 1876; *SLPD*, January 18, 1877.
19. *SLR*, August 11, 1876; *SLPD*, January 18, 1877.
20. *SLR*, August 11, 1876.
21. *SLR*, August 11, 1876.
22. *SLR*, August 26, 1876, quoting *WB*.
23. *SLR*, September 1, 1876.
24. *SLR*, September 1, 1876.
25. *SLR*, September 1, 1876; *SLPD*, January 18, 1877.
26. *SLR*, September 1, 1876.
27. *SLGD*, October 16, 1876; *SLPD*, October 20, 1876.
28. *SLGD*, October 31, 1876; *SLPD*, January 18, 1877.
29. *SLGD*, November 24, 1876; *SLPD*, January 18, 1877.
30. *JCT*, December 8, 1876; *SLGD*, December 18, 1876, quoting *WB*.
31. *SLGD*, December 18, 1876, quoting *WB*.

32. *SLGD*, December 18, 1876, quoting *WB*.
33. *SLGD*, December 18, 1876, quoting *WB*.
34. *SLGD*, December 18, 1876, quoting *WB*.
35. MSPD.
36. *SLPD*, January 18, 1877.
37. MSPD; *WB*, April 18, 1882.

3. Alice Dyke: Cold-Blooded Murderer or Self-Defender?

38. *KCT*, July 31, 1887; *KCJ*, July 31, 1887; *KCJ*, August 2, 1887.
39. *KCT*, July 31, 1887.
40. *KCT*, July 31, 1887; *KCJ*, July 31, 1887.
41. *KCJ*, July 31, 1887.
42. *KCJ*, July 31, 1887.
43. *KCJ*, July 31, 1887; *KCT*, July 31, 1887.
44. *KCJ*, July 31, 1887.
45. *KCJ*, July 31, 1887.
46. *KCT*, July 31, 1887; *KCJ*, July 31, 1887.
47. *KCJ*, August 1, 1887.
48. *KCJ*, August 1, 1887.
49. *KCJ*, August 1, 1887.
50. *KCJ*, August 2, 1877.
51. *KCJ*, September 16, 1887; *KCJ*, September 20, 1887.
52. *KCJ*, October 19, 1887; *KCJ*, October 21, 1887.
53. *KCJ*, October 21, 1887.
54. *KCJ*, October 21, 1887.
55. *KCS*, October 21, 1887.
56. *KCS*, October 21, 1887; *KCJ*, October 22, 1887; *KCT*, July 21, 1892.
57. *KCS*, October 21, 1887; *KCJ*, October 22, 1887.
58. *KCJ*, October 22, 1887.
59. *KCJ*, October 22, 1887.
60. *KCJ*, October 22, 1887.
61. *KCJ*, October 22, 1887.
62. *KCJ*, October 23, 1887; *KCJ*, October 25, 1887; *KCS*, October 24, 1887.
63. *KCS*, October 24, 1887; *KCS*, October 27, 1887; *KCS*, December 8, 1887; *KCS*, December 13, 1887; *KCJ*, December 9, 1887; *KCJ*, December 15, 1887; *KCT*, December 15, 1887.
64. *KCT*, February 3, 1888; MSPD.

65. *KCT*, November 27, 1888; *KCT*, November 28, 1888.
66. *KCJ*, November 28, 1888.
67. *KCT*, November 29, 1888.
68. *KCS*, January 10, 1889.
69. *KCT*, April 14, 1889; *KCT*, April 20, 1889.
70. *KCJ*, September 14, 1889; *KCJ*, September 17, 1889.
71. *KCS*, July 29, 1890.

4. "Kill the Son of a Bitch": The Story of Blanche Connors

72. *KCS*, December 26, 1887.
73. *KCS*, December 26, 1887; *KCJ*, February 18, 1888.
74. *KCS*, December 26, 1887; *KCS*, December 29, 1887.
75. *KCS*, December 26, 1887.
76. *KCS*, December 29, 1887.
77. *KCS*, December 29, 1887; *KCJ*, December 29, 1887.
78. *KCS*, February 14, 1888; *KCS*, February 21, 1888.
79. *KCS*, February 23, 1888; *KCS*, April 17, 1888; *KCJ*, April 18, 1888.
80. *KCJ*, April 21, 1888; *KCT*, April 21, 1888.
81. *KCS*, April 21, 1888; *KCS*, April 23, 1888; *KCJ*, April 24, 1888.
82. *KCT*, April 24, 1888.
83. *KCT*, April 24, 1888.
84. *KCT*, April 24, 1888.
85. *KCT*, April 24, 1888.
86. *KCT*, April 24, 1888.
87. *KCT*, April 25, 1888.
88. *KCS*, July 4, 1888.
89. *KCS*, August 1, 1888
90. *KCJ*, February 1, 1899; *KCT*, February 27, 1889.
91. *KCS*, April 18, 1889, *KCJ*, April 19, 1889.
92. *KCJ*, June 3, 1890; MSPD.

5. "I Have Killed Pete": Maud Lewis Murders Her Lover

93. *SLGD*, May 14, 1895.
94. *SLGD*, May 14, 1895.
95. *SLGD*, May 14, 1895.

96. *SLGD*, May 14, 1895.
97. *SLGD*, May 14, 1895; *SLGD*, 16, 1895.
98. *SLGD*, May 14, 1895.
99. *SLGD*, May 14, 1895.
100. *SLGD*, May 14, 1895; *SLPD*, May 15, 1895.
101. *SLGD*, May 14, 1895.
102. *SLGD*, May 24, 1895.
103. *SLPD*, May 26, 1895.
104. *SLGD*, June 15, 1895; *SLPD*, June 15, 1895.
105. *SLPD*, July 26, 1895.
106. *SLPD*, July 26, 1895.
107. *SLPD*, July 26, 1895.
108. *SLPD*, July 26, 1895.
109. *SLPD*, July 26, 1895.
110. *SLPD*, July 26, 1895.
111. *SLPD*, July 26, 1895.
112. *SLPD*, May 15, 1895; Missouri Marriages, familysearch.org; U.S. Census, 1870, 1880.
113. *SLGD*, August 15, 1895; *SLPD*, August 15, 1895.
114. *SLGD*, August 15, 1895; *SLGD*, September 8, 1895.
115. *SLPD*, October 16–18, 1895.
116. *SLPD*, October 20, 1895.
117. *SLPD*, October 20, 1895; "Peter R. Morrissey (1859–1895)," https://politicalgraveyard.com.
118. *SLPD*, October 27, 1895; *SLPD*, November 2, 1895.
119. *SLPD*, January 7, 1896; *SLPD*, January 12, 1896; *SLGD*, November 20, 1896; *SLGD*, November 21, 1896.
120. *SLGD*, January 29, 1898; MSPD; Maud Lewis, Pardons and Commutations, Box 69, Folder 4.

6. A Shotgun Wedding Turns Deadly: The Story of Lulu Prince

121. *KCT*, December 5, 1900; *KCJ*, January 11, 1901; U.S. Census, 1900.
122. *KCT*, December 5, 1900.
123. *KCT*, December 5, 1900.
124. *KCT*, December 5, 1900.
125. *KCT*, December 5, 1900.
126. *KCT*, January 9, 1901.

127. *KCT*, January 9, 1901.
128. *KCT*, January 11, 1901; *KCT*, January 13, 1901; *KCS*, January 11, 1901; *KCJ*, January 11, 1901.
129. *KCT*, January 11, 1901; *KCT*, January 13, 1901; *KCS*, January 11, 1901; *KCJ*, January 11, 1901.
130. *KCT*, January 11, 1901; *KCS*, January 11, 1901; *KCJ*, January 11, 1901.
131. *KCJ*, January 11, 1901.
132. *KCJ*, January 11, 1901; *KCT*, January 11, 1901.
133. *KCS*, January 11, 1901.
134. *KCS*, January 11, 1901.
135. *KCJ*, January 11, 1901.
136. *KCJ*, January 13, 1901.
137. *KCJ*, January 13, 1901.
138. *KCJ*, January 13, 1901.
139. *KCJ*, January 13, 1901.
140. *KCJ*, January 13, 1901.
141. *KCJ*, January 23, 1901; *KCJ*, January 24, 1901; *KCJ*, February 16, 1901; *KCS*, February 18, 1901.
142. *KCS*, March 1, 1901; *KCT*, March 30, 1901.
143. *KCT*, June 3, 1901.
144. *KCJ*, June 3, 1901.
145. *KCT*, June 6, 1891.
146. *KCT*, June 6, 1891.
147. *KCS*, June 6, 1901.
148. *KCS*, June 6, 1901.
149. *KCT*, Jun 8–16, 1901.
150. *KCT*, June 16, 1901.
151. *KCT*, June 17, 1901.
152. *KCJ*, July 31, 1901; *KCJ*, August 22, 1901; *KCJ*, September 6, 1901.
153. *KCJ*, February 13, 1902.
154. *KCJ*, July 4, 1903; *KCJ*, August 21, 1903; State v. Kennedy.
155. *KCS*, January 10, 1904.
156. *KCT*, January 26, 1904.
157. *KCT*, January 26–28, 1904; *KCJ*, January 28, 1904.
158. *KCS*, January 28, 1904.
159. *KCJ*, January 30, 1904.
160. *OT*, March 5, 1904.

7. Always the Smile: The Remorseless Aggie Myers

161. *KCS*, May 11, 1904.
162. *KCS*, May 11–12, 1904.
163. *KCS*, May 12, 1905; *KCJ*, May 12, 1904.
164. *KCS*, May 11–12, 1904.
165. *KCS*, May 12, 1904.
166. *KCJ*, May 13, 1904.
167. *KCJ*, May 13, 1904.
168. *KCS*, May 20, 1904.
169. *KCS*, May 27, 1904; *KCS*, July 4, 1904; *KCJ*, July 5, 1904; *KCT*, July 5, 1904.
170. *KCJ*, July 6, 1904.
171. *KCS*, July 6, 1904.
172. *KCJ*, July 7, 1904.
173. *KCS*, July 7, 1904.
174. *KCS*, July 9, 1904; *KCS*, July 10, 1904,
175. *KCS*, July 12, 1904; *KCT*, July 14, 1904.
176. *KCJ*, July 16, 1904; *KCS*, July 16, 1904.
177. *KCS*, August 1, 1904.
178. *KCS*, August 1, 1904.
179. *KCS*, January 13, 1905.
180. *KCJ*, January 14, 1905.
181. *KCS*, March 22, 1905; *KCJ*, June 8, 1905.
182. *KCJ*, June 9–11, 1905.
183. *KCJ*, June 11–12, 1905.
184. *KCJ*, June 25, 1905; *KCJ*, May 23, 1906.
185. *KCJ*, May 30, 1906; *KCJ*, June 20, 1906.
186. *KCJ*, August 28, 1906; *KCT*, October 3, 1906.
187. *KCJ*, July 4, 1906; *KCJ*, October 9, 1906; *KCJ*, October 19, 1906.
188. *KCJ*, December 7, 1906; *KCJ*, December 9, 1906.
189. *KCJ*, January 5, 1907; *KCJ*, January 10, 1907; *KCS*, January 7, 1907.
190. *KCJ*, January 5, 1907; *KCS*, January 7, 1907; *KCT*, April 9, 1907.
191. *KCS*, April 19, 1907; MSPD.
192. *KCS*, September 19, 1923; *KCS*, January 9, 1925; *KCS*, January 11, 1925; *KCS*, December 8, 1929.

8. Almost Like a Tigress: The Story of Annie Hunning

193. *SLPD*, December 10, 1911; U.S. Census, 1910.
194. *SLPD*, December 10, 1911.
195. *SLPD*, December 10, 1911.
196. *SLPD*, December 10, 1911.
197. *SLPD*, December 11, 1911.
198. *SLPD*, December 11–12, 1911.
199. *SLPD*, December 11, 1911.
200. *SLST*, December 13, 1911.
201. *SLST*, December 13, 1911.
202. *SLPD*, December 15, 1911.
203. *SLPD*, December 15, 1911.
204. *SLGD*, December 15, 1911; *SLPD*, December 15, 1911.
205. *SLPD*, December 18, 1911.
206. *SLPD*, December 19, 1911; *SLGD*, December 20, 1911.
207. *SLGD*, December 20, 1911.
208. *SLST*, December 21, 1911.
209. *SLST*, December 25, 1911.
210. *SLST*, December 25, 1911.
211. *SLST*, December 25, 1911.
212. *SLGD*, December 26, 1911.
213. *SLST*, December 26, 1911.
214. *SLGD*, December 30, 1911.
215. *SLGD*, December 30–31, 1911.
216. *SLST*, January 17, 1912; *SLGD*, January 17, 1912.
217. *SLGD*, January 3, 1912; *SLST*, January 16–17, 1912.
218. *SLST*, January 16, 1912.
219. *SLST*, January 17, 1912.
220. *SLST*, January 29, 1912; *SLST*, January 31, 1912; *SLPD*, April 1–3, 1912.
221. *SLPD*, April 9, 1912.
222. *SLPD*, April 10, 1912.
223. *SLPD*, April 11–12, 1912.
224. *SLST*, May 17, 1912; *SLST*, May 19, 1912; *SLST*, May 21, 1912; *SLST*, May 22, 1912.
225. MSPD; Anna Hunning, Pardons and Commutations, Box 114, Folder 6e.

9. Clara Schweiger of Spotted Adder Snake Fame

226. *KCS*, May 1, 1915; *KCS*, May 2, 1915.
227. *KCP*, November 12, 1914; *KCS*, March 3, 1916.
228. *KCP*, May 1, 1915; *KCS*, May 2, 1915.
229. *KCP*, November 11, 1914.
230. *KCP*, November 11, 1914.
231. *KCP*, November 11, 12, 1914.
232. *KCP*, November 28, 1914; *KCP*, January 13, 1915; *KCS*, November 28, 1914; *KCJ*, November 29, 1914.
233. *KCS*, May 2, 1915.
234. *KCS*, May 2, 1915.
235. *KCP*, May 1, 1915.
236. *KCP*, May 1, 1915.
237. *KCP*, May 1, 1915.
238. *KCP*, May 1, 1915; *KCS*, May 2, 1915; *KCJ*, May 3, 1915.
239. *KCP*, May 1, 1915.
240. *KCP*, May 1, 1915.
241. *KCS*, May 1, 1915.
242. *KCS*, May 2, 1915.
243. *KCS*, May 2, 1915.
244. *KCS*, May 2, 1915.
245. *KCS*, May 2, 1915; *KCP*, May 3, 1915.
246. *KCP*, May 3, 1915.
247. *KCP*, May 3, 1915.
248. *KCP*, May 4, 1915; *KCJ*, May 4–5, 1915.
249. *KCP*, June 5, 1915; KCP, June 12, 1915; *KCP*, August 2, 1915; *KCP*, October 25, 1915; *KCP*, January 10, 1916; *KCS*, November 15, 1915; *KCS*, February 29, 1916.
250. *KCT*, March 2, 1916.
251. *KCS*, March 2, 1916.
252. *KCS*, March 3, 1916; *KCJ*, March 4, 1916.
253. *KCJ*, March 4, 1916.
254. *KCJ*, March 8, 1916; *KCS*, March 8, 1916.
255. *KCS*, April 1, 1916; *KCS*, April 3, 1916; *KCS*, April 9, 1916; *KCS*, October 13, 1916; *KCP*, June 22, 1916.
256. *KCS*, February 12, 1918; *KCS*, March 6, 1918; MSPD; Clara T. Schweiger, Pardons and Commutations, Box 117, Folder 6g.

10. I Showed Him the Road: The Story of Mary Appleby

257. *SL*, November 13, 1921.
258. *SL*, November 10, 1921; Find a Grave, Memorial 160487760.
259. *SL*, November 10, 1921; *SMR*, November 10, 1921.
260. *SL*, November 10, 1921.
261. *SMR*, November 10, 1921.
262. *SL*, January 5, 1922.
263. *SL*, November 10, 1921.
264. *SL*, November 13, 1921; *SL*, January 5, 1922.
265. *SL*, November 10, 1921.
266. *SL*, January 5, 1922.
267. *SL*, November 10, 1921.
268. *SL*, January 5, 1922.
269. *SL*, January 5, 1922.
270. *SL*, November 10, 1921; *SL*, January 5, 1922.
271. *SMR*, November 10, 1921.
272. *SMR*, November 10, 1921.
273. *SL*, November 10, 1921.
274. *SL*, November 11, 13, 1921.
275. *SL*, November 17, 1921.
276. *SL*, November 17, 1921.
277. *SL*, November 18, 1921; *SL*, December 2, 1921.
278. *SL*, January 4, 1922.
279. *SL*, January 5, 1922.
280. *SL*, January 6, 1922
281. *SL*, April 7, 1922; *SMR*, April 8, 1922.
282. *SMR*, April 9, 1922.
283. *SMR*, June 1, 1922.
284. *MNR*, June 12, 1929; *MNR*, February 16, 1941; Find a Grave, Memorial #160487760.

11. An Honorable Girl: The Story of Ada Lee Biggs

285. *FN*, November 16, 1928.
286. *SLPD*, July 17, 1928.
287. *SLPD*, July 17, 1928.
288. *SLPD*, November 14, 1928.

289. *SLPD*, November 14, 1928.
290. *SLPD*, November 14, 1928; *SLST*, November 14, 1928.
291. *SLPD*, July 17, 1928; *SLST*, November 14, 1928.
292. *SLPD*, July 17, 1928.
293. *SLPD*, July 17, 1928.
294. *SLPD*, July 17, 1928.
295. *FN*, July 20, 1928.
296. *FN*, July 20, 1928.
297. *FN*, July 20, 1928.
298. *FN*, July 20, 1928.
299. *SLPD*, July 17, 1928.
300. *SLPD*, July 17, 1928.
301. *SLST*, July 17, 1928.
302. *SLST*, July 17, 1928.
303. *SLST*, July 17, 1928.
304. *SLPD*, July 17, 1928.
305. *SLPD*, November 15, 1928.
306. *SLPD*, November 15, 1928.
307. *SLPD*, November 15, 1928.
308. *SLPD*, November 15, 1928.
309. *SLPD*, November 15, 1928.
310. MSPD.

12. "I Have Killed Him and I'm Glad I Did": The Story of LaCulia Curry

311. *SLA*, July 17, 1931.
312. *SLA*, July 17, 1931; *SLPD*, July 1, 1931.
313. *SLA*, July 17, 1931; *SLA*, January 22, 1932; *SLGD*, July 16, 1931; *KCC*, January 29, 1932.
314. *SLA*, July 17, 1931; *SLPD*, July 16, 1931.
315. *SLA*, July 24, 1931.
316. *SLA*, July 24, 1931.
317. *KCC*, January 29, 1932; *SLA*, January 22, 1932.
318. *KCC*, January 29, 1932.
319. *KCC*, January 29, 1932.
320. *SLA*, January 22 and 29, 1932.
321. *SLA*, January 29, 1932.

322. *SLA*, March 5, 1937; *SLA*, January 6, 1961; "LaCulia Curry," Pardons and Commutations, Box 155, Folder 8i.

13. Virgil Reece Takes the Gate: The Story of Gertrude Lytle

323. U.S. Census, 1910, 1920; "Luella E. Jamison," Wiki Tree; Arkansas Marriage License Search, Craighead County.
324. *SJG*, June 28, 1932.
325. *SJNP*, March 15, 1930.
326. *SJNP*, March 15, 1930; *SJG*, June 28, 1932.
327. *SJNP*, June 28, 1932.
328. *SJNP*, June 28, 1932.
329. *SJG*, June 28, 1932; U.S. Census, 1930.
330. *SJNP*, June 28, 1932.
331. *SJNP*, June 28, 1932.
332. *SJNP*, June 28, 1932.
333. *SJNP*, June 28, 1932.
334. *SJG*, June 28, 1932.
335. *SJNP*, June 28, 1932.
336. *SJG*, June 28, 1932.
337. *SRACD*, July 1, 1932.
338. *SJG*, June 28, 1932.
339. *SJG*, June 28, 1932.
340. *SJNP*, June 28, 1932; *KCT*, June 28, 1932; *SRACD*, July 1, 1932.
341. *SJG*, June 28, 1932.
342. *SRACD*, July 1, 1932.
343. *SJG*, June 28, 1932.
344. *SJNP*, June 28–29, 1932.
345. *SRACD*, November 25, 1932; *SJG*, November 22–24, 1932; *SJNP*, November 22–23, 1932.
346. *SRACD*, November 25, 1932; *SJG*, November 24, 1932.
347. *SJNP*, February 17, 1933; "Gertrude Graham, about 1902–16 July 1946."
348. *SRACD*, May 21, 1943; *SJG*, June 28, 1932.

14. Bonnie Parker: The Auburn-Haired Bandit Queen

349. Milner, *Life and Times*, 51–52.
350. Milner, 51-52; *JNH*, November 30, 1932; *JG*, December 1, 1932.
351. *JG*, December 1, 1932; *JNH*, November 30, 1932.
352. Milner, *Life and Times*, 52–61.
353. *SP*, January 27, 1933.
354. *SP*, January 27, 1933.
355. *SP*, January 27, 1933.
356. *SP*, January 27, 1933.
357. *SP*, January 27, 1933.
358. *SP*, January 27, 1933.
359. *SP*, January 27, 1933; *SL*, January 27, 1933.
360. *SP*, January 27, 1933.
361. *SP*, January 27, 1933.
362. Guinn, *Go Down Together*, 163–64; Barrow, *My Life*, 40.
363. Guinn, *Go Down Together*, 165–67; Barrow, *My Life*, 44–46.
364. Barrow, *My Life*, 48–49: Guinn, *Go Down Together*, 166–67.
365. *JG*, April 14, 1933; Barrow, *My Life*, 49–51.
366. Guinn, *Go Down Together*, 170; *JG*, April 14, 1933.
367. *JG*, April 14–15, 1933; Milner, *Life and Times*, 66; Guinn, *Go Down Together*, 109–10, 171–76.
368. *KCJ*, July 20, 1933; Guinn, *Go Down Together*, 177–208, 215–17.
369. Guinn, *Go Down Together*, 234–62.
370. *SDN*, February 13, 1933; *SLP*, February 13, 1933; *GSCNO*, February 14, 1933.
371. *SDN*, January 20, 1970.
372. *TT*, April 7, 1934; *SJ*, May 23, 1934.

15. A Triangular Love Tangle: The Story of Ima Gaskin

373. *HMH*, June 22, 1934; U.S. Census, 1930.
374. *HMH*, June 22, 1934; *BCN*, June 16, 1934; *PBDAR*, June 21, 1934.
375. *CDA*, June 21–22, 1934; *PBDAR*, August 10, 1934.
376. *CDA*, June 19, 1934; *PBDAR*, June 16, 1934; U.S. Census, 1930.
377. *CDA*, June 21–22, 1934.
378. *CDA*, June 21–22, 1934; *HMH*, June 22, 1934.
379. *PBDAR*, August 11, 1934.
380. *CDA*, August 14, 1934; *PBDAR*, August 10–11, 1934.

381. *PBDAR*, August 11, 1934.
382. *PBDAR*, August 11, 1934; *CDA*, August 14, 1934.
383. *PBDAR*, August 11, 1934.
384. *CDA*, August 11, 1934; *HMH*, September 21, 1934; Register of Prisoners.

16. The Mysterious Death of Grover Myers

385. *GS*, April 20, 1939.
386. *PBDAR*, May 8, 1939.
387. *GNR*, June 16, 1923; *GNR*, June 19, 1923.
388. *PBDAR*, May 8, 1939.
389. *PBDAR*, May 6, 1939.
390. *PBDAR*, May 6, 1939.
391. *FDN*, May 11, 1939.
392. *FDN*, May 11, 1939.
393. *FDN*, May 11, 1939.
394. *FDN*, May 11, 1939.
395. *FDN*, May 11, 1939.
396. *PBDAR*, May 8, 1939.
397. *GS*, May 11, 1939.
398. *PBDAR*, May 11, 1939.
399. *PBDAR*, May 29, 1939; *PBDAR*, June 7, 1939; *PBDAR*, July 8, 1939.
400. *GS*, August 17, 1939; Register of Prisoners.
401. *PBDAR*, October 2, 1940; Register of Prisoners.

17. Self-Defense or Murder? The Story of Iva Holden

402. *HH*, August 22, 1963; *SLP*, August 22, 1963.
403. *HH*, August 22, 1963.
404. *HH*, August 22, 1963.
405. *HH*, August 22, 1963; *SDN*, August 23, 1963.
406. *SLP*, August 22, 1963.
407. *SLP*, August 22, 1963.
408. *SLP*, September 15, 1963; *HH*, September 19, 1963.
409. *SLP*, February 12, 1964.
410. *SLP*, February 12, 1964.
411. *SLP*, February 12, 1964.

412. *SLP*, February 12, 1964; *HH*, August 22, 1963.
413. *SLP*, February 12, 1964.
414. *SLP*, February 12, 1964.
415. *HH*, February 13, 1964.
416. *SLP*, April 22, 1965.

18. Forty Years Behind Bars for a Crime She Didn't Commit?

417. Justice for Patty Prewitt, "Update: Patty Is Home."
418. *KCS*, February 18–19, 1984; *KCS*, March 4, 1984.
419. *KCS*, February 18, 19, 1984.
420. *KCS*, March 4, 1984.
421. *KCS*, February 23, 1984; *KCS*, March 4, 1984.
422. *KCS*, March 4, 1984.
423. *KCS*, March 4, 1984; *KCS*, April 6, 1984.
424. *KCS*, April 6, 1984.
425. *KCS*, April 6, 1984; *KCS*, April 10, 1984.
426. *KCS*, April 16, 1985.
427. *KCS*, April 16–17, 1985.
428. *KCS*, April 17, 1985.
429. *KCS*, April 17, 1985.
430. *KCS*, April 19,1985.
431. *KCS*, April 19, 1985; Justice for Patty Prewitt, "Deeply Flawed Trial."
432. *PBDAR*, April 29, 1986; *KCS*, April 30, 1986.
433. Justice for Patty Prewitt, "An Inspiration to Generations."

19. "Honey, Eve's Here": The Story of Evelyn Shire

434. *SNL*, August 9, 1988; *SNL*, December 9, 1989.
435. *SNL*, December 9, 1989.
436. *SNL*, December 9, 1989.
437. *SNL*, August 9, 1988; *SNL*, December 6, 1989.
438. *SNL*, August 8–9, 1988; *SNL*, November 2, 1988; *SNL*, November 22, 1988.
439. *SNL*, May 2, 1989.
440. *SNL*, August 3, 1989; *SNL*, December 5, 1989.
441. State v. Shire.
442. *SNL*, December 9, 1989.

443. *SNL*, December 9, 1989.
444. *SNL*, December 9, 1989.
445. State v. Shire.

20. "I Won't Take That Anymore": Debra Carson and the Battered Woman Syndrome

446. *SJNPG*, July 12, 1989; *SJNPG*, September 27, 1990.
447. *SJNPG*, September 27, 1990.
448. *SJNPG*, September 27, 1990; *BRC*, July 19, 1989.
449. *SJNPG*, July 12, 1989.
450. *SJNPG*, July 13, 1989; *SJNPG*, November 18, 1989; *KCT*, August 7, 1989.
451. *KCT*, August 7, 1989.
452. *KCT*, August 7, 1989.
453. *KCT*, August 7, 1989.
454. *KCT*, August 7, 1989.
455. *KCT*, August 7, 1989.
456. *KCT*, August 7, 1989.
457. *KCT*, August 7, 1989.
458. *SJNPG*, November 18, 1989.
459. *SJNPG*, September 27, 1990.
460. *SJNPG*, September 27, 1990.
461. *SJNPG*, September 28, 1990.
462. *SJNPG*, September 28, 1990.
463. *SJNPG*, September 28, 1990.
464. *SJNPG*, September 29, 1990.

BIBLIOGRAPHY

Arkansas Marriage License Search. Craighead County. https://marriage.cisarkansas.com.

Barrow, Blanche Caldwell. *My Life with Bonnie and Clyde*. Edited by John Neal Phillips. University of Oklahoma Press, 2004.

Family Search. "Gertrude Graham, about 1902–16 July 1946." https://ancestors.familysearch.org.

———. "Missouri Marriages, 1750–1920." https://www.familysearch.org.

———. "United States Census Online Genealogy Records." https://www.familysearch.org.

Guinn, Jeff. *Go Down Together: The True, Untold Story of Bonnie and Clyde.* Simon and Schuster, 2009.

Justice for Patty Prewitt. "A Deeply Flawed Trial." https://pattyprewitt.com.

———. "An Inspiration to Generations of Women Behind Bars." https://pattyprewitt.com.

———. "Update: Patty Is Home." https://pattyprewitt.com.

Milner, E.R. *The Life and Times of Bonnie and Clyde*. Southern Illinois University Press, 1996.

Missouri State Penitentiary Database, Missouri State Archives, https://s1.sos.mo.gov.

Pardons and Commutations. Missouri State Archives. Jefferson City, Missouri.

The Political Graveyard. "Peter R. Morrissey (1859–1895)." https://politicalgraveyard.com.

Register of Prisoners. Missouri State Archives. Jefferson City, Missouri.

State v. Kennedy. Missouri Supreme Court Reports, v. 177, April Term 1903. Missouri Digital Heritage. https://mdh.contentdm.oclc.org.

State v. Shire. Justia Law. https://law.justia.com.

WikiTree. "Luella E. Jamison." https://www.wikitree.com.

INDEX

D

E

F

G

H

I

J

K

L

M

N

O

P

R

S

T

V

W

ABOUT THE AUTHOR

Larry Wood is a retired public schoolteacher and a freelance writer specializing in the history of Missouri and the Ozarks. He has authored over twenty-five nonfiction history books, including ten previous titles published by The History Press. Wood has also published six western/historical novels and over five hundred magazine articles and stories. He is an honorary lifetime member of the Missouri Writers' Guild and the current president of the Ozarks Writers' League. You can connect with him on his website at https://www.larrywoodauthor.com/ or follow him on Facebook at https://www.facebook.com/AuthorLarryWood/. He also maintains a blog on regional history at www.ozarks-history.blogspot.com.

Visit us at
www.historypress.com